Endorsements for Three Commands

You know those wonderful stories of idyllic, trauma-free childhoods that lead to healthy and problem-free lives? Well, that's not the story of Bruce Pagano II. Pain crashed into his life early and left him struggling to understand true love as an adult. In *Three Commands*, he shares his experience with vulnerability and insight about how he moved from striving for approval to resting in God's love. By unpacking the biblical definition of love he equips readers to serve, not out of an insecurity of whether they are loved, but from an assurance that they truly are.

Drew Dyck, editor and author of *Your Future Self Will Thank You: Secrets to Self-control from the Bible and Brain Science.*

If you are at all disillusioned by modern Christian interpretations of caring for the hurt and brokenness in our world... This book is a light in the darkness.

Chaplain Thomas Hogan, Catmon CEBU, Philippines

What did Jesus mean when He said "Love one another?" This book explores the deeper meaning of that command AND how to practically live that out in everyday life!

Pastor Grant Clark, West Jordan, UT

Using parts of his own story Bruce shares the heart of being kingdom people, which the American church needs to hear.

Kyle Altenbern, Parma, ID

Three Commands
Jesus' Fulfillment of the Law through Love

BRUCE PAGANO II

Ink Publishing House, LLC.

Copyright © 2020, Ink Publishing House LLC. All Rights Reserved.

Three Commands: Jesus' Fulfillment of the Law through Love by Bruce Pagano II

Printed in the United States of America

ISBN-13: 978-0-578-65454-6

No part of this document may be reproduced or transmitted in any form or by any means, electronic, mechanical, photocopying, recording, or otherwise, without prior written permission of the author.

Requests for permission to make copies of any part of the work should be submitted to Ink Publishing House at inkpubhouse@gmail.com or Bruce Pagano II at bruce@brucepagano.com.

Unless otherwise noted, all Scripture quotations are taken from the Holman Christian Standard Bible®, Used by Permission HCSB ©1999, 2000, 2002, 2003, 2009 Holman Bible Publishers. Holman Christian Standard Bible®, Holman CSB®, and HCSB® are federally registered trademarks of Holman Bible Publishers.

For those scriptures identified as ESV:
The Holy Bible, English Standard Version® (ESV®), Copyright © 2001 by Crossway, a publishing ministry of Good News Publishers.
All rights reserved. ESV Text Edition: 2016

Cover: Peter O'Connor, Bespoke Book Covers, www.bespokebookcovers.com
Book Design: Ink Publishing House LLC, www.inkpublishinghouse.com
Author photo by Sarah Pagano, www.sarahpagano.photography

Disclaimer: The material in this book cannot substitute for professional advice; further, the author is not liable if the reader relied on the material and was financially damaged in some way, and the recollection of stories shared are recalled to the best of the author's knowledge.

DEDICATION

To my wife, Sarah. Thank you for helping me to learn what it means to love well.

APPRECIATIONS

I HAD ORIGINALLY DEDICATED this book to multiple people. Then, Drew Dyck, author of *Your Future Self will Thank You* and editor at Moody Publishing, tweeted out that dedicating a book to multiple people is a cop out. I really respect Drew and his take on things, but his tweet was a huge problem for me because I really do owe the content of this book to a whole bunch of people. Initially I decided to ignore his tweet, because Twitter is typically an incubator for intentional conflict, so I pretended that Drew was just trying to provoke mass chaos among the writing world. Unfortunately, I've been following him for long enough and have heard him speak enough times that I knew he was being serious. I legitimately lamented over it of a few weeks.

Then, about a month later, I remembered that "acknowledgements" are a real thing in books. So I decided to change my multiple dedications to acknowledgements, or appreciations. This is me, acknowledging the people who were instrumental in helping me form and refine all of the ideas that built this book.

I want to start by acknowledge my God. Thank you for being a God who loves us through our mess-ups, walks us into greater understanding of love, and places people in the lives of His children to demonstrate a love that reveals you.

Next, I want to thank my family. I already dedicated the entire book to my wife, but there's so much more that could have been said on that page. And to my children: James, Andrew, Malachi, and Hazel. There was a time when I didn't understand what it meant to love well. And even when I had some idea, I didn't always do it well. It was during those times that I knew I wasn't as good of a father as I wanted to be. Thank you for your patience and allowing me to figure out what it means to actually live out loving others. My heart was always aimed toward loving you well, even if I fell short at times. Thank you to all of you, my wife and kids, for helping me understand what loving well was always meant to look like. The amount of grace you offered is nothing short of divine. Thank you for your love.

And then there are all the people who make up my tribe. Thank you to all of you, both past and present. Over the years my tribe has taken on various forms, but all of you have been instrumental in helping me understand the nuts and bolts of this love thing. Thank you to the members of theSHIFT, NCC Kingstowne, Awaken church, and my home group peeps (Daniel &

Bailey, Nic and Allie, and Chris). You have all been a vital part to my growing in understanding of what Jesus meant when He said, "love each other." Thank you for loving well.

And lastly, while there are a lot of writers, authors, and teachers that I admire and who have influenced me, I do actually want to acknowledge Drew. Thanks for calling me out, even if indirectly, and helping me to realize the best way to organize a book dedication and acknowledgements sections. Thanks for being just a really funny, but thoughtful, guy and great writer; you continuously inspire me to work harder on my craft. And thanks for the endorsement; it means a lot. Thanks Drew.

TABLE OF CONTENTS

My Invitation. Looking For Love And Finding Jesus — 1

Part One. What Is Love — 15

Chapter 1. God is Love — 17

Chapter 2. The Law and Love — 27

Chapter 3. He First Loved Us — 47

Part Two. Who We Love — 65

Chapter 4. A New Way to Love — 67

Chapter 5. The Greatest Command — 81

Chapter 6. The Second Command — 95

Part Three. Why We Love — 111

Chapter 7. To Spur Each Other On — 115

Chapter 8. To Go and Make Disciples — 129

Chapter 9. To Go and Do the Same — 159

His Invitation. Finding Love and Looking for Others — 177

Notes — 179

"...ο Θεός είναι αγάπη"

1 Ιωάννης 4:8

"...God is Love"

1 John 4:8

My Invitation

LOOKING FOR LOVE AND FINDING JESUS

The biggest disease this day and age is that of people feeling unloved.
~ Princess Diana ~

"I'M DONE. With as hard as I've tried and worked and with everything I've done, you let this happen?! I'm done doing this and I won't anymore!" That was my response, in the early part of September 2008, to finding out my wife wanted a divorce. Only, I didn't say it to her; I said it to God. I actually said it out loud. I wanted to make sure He heard me. Belief in God wasn't an issue for me, so speaking out loud to Him was natural. In fact, I was confident enough in my belief in His existence that even at this, my rock bottom, I just couldn't get to whatever point is needed to abandon that belief. Abandoning my relationship with Him seemed easier than abandoning belief in Him, so that's what I chose to do.

I sat in the living room that night convinced I had been a good Christian. I went to church, I made sure my family went to church despite the tension it caused with my wife, I read the Bible, I had almost completely stopped cussing, and I even attended a Bible study for married couples. What more could God want from me? I often felt guilty about my behavior, routinely confessed and asking for forgiveness for the bad stuff I did. Surely that showed my commitment to God's set of Christian values. As far as I was concerned I had committed 20 years to being a good Christian. Why was that not enough? Why did it not matter to Him? Why was He letting my marriage fall apart? How could *He* let this happen?

In the process of losing my marriage, I also felt like I was losing God, even though that loss was my decision. And in the aftermath of cutting away major parts of my identity – 'husband' and 'Christian' – questions automatically arose that involved examining my faith and belief system. Up to that point, I had identified as a Christian for 20 years. But as I explored those questions, I started to discover that I didn't really have any idea what being a Christian meant. A large part of that was realizing my complete misunderstanding of Jesus and ignorance of what He said and did.

To be honest, Jesus was just a peripheral element of my religion. He was necessary to get to God, but after that I didn't have a lot of understanding, or quite frankly need to involve Him in my Christianity. I know, Christianity literally has the word *Christ* in it, but I never had anyone actually disciple me into that place of understanding. Because of that, most of my focus was directed toward pleasing the Father, which is ultimately impossible from a human standpoint, as seen by thousands of years of Israelite attempts and failures. At the very least I wanted to avoid making Him angry, which, to be honest, seemed like something I was not very good at. The one thing I did know, and had heard often, was that He was a loving Father and not only that, but He actually *was* love. I had no clue what that meant and genuinely doubted that I had ever experienced love from Him. My lack of understanding undergirded the belief that His love wasn't meant for me and that somehow I didn't deserve it. The crumbling of my marriage was just further evidence of how unworthy of His love I was.

Eventually, I came to understand that I had never really known what genuine love was and that I had spent most of my life looking for it. What a bleak realization for a 32-year-old, soon to be divorced and single father. What's worse was that I had spent 20 years as a "Christian" and had no idea where to even start learning what love was, let alone what it meant to be loved.

CAPTURED BY LOVE

I never intended for this book to be longer than nine chapters. When I started I liked the idea of three neat parts, each with three chapters. It was symmetrical and made me feel like it was somehow balanced. When I finished writing my perfectly symmetrical first draft, I gave it to nine people to read.

One of my readers was my friend Adam. I mention him later in the book, but he's a pastor of both my church and my heart. He's one of the guys that God used to show me that there are vocational pastors who focus on loving others well, rather than just the business of church as an organization. After he read the first chapter, *God is Love*, we met for coffee so he could share some thoughts. The first thing he told me was that it was a great chapter and that he learned a lot. Then he asked me why I wrote the book. I wasn't sure if, outside of an editor, I had ever had anyone ask me that. Of course I've offered up my reasons for writing to others, but no one had ever asked me for a pointed purpose. After I gave it some thought and shared some reasons,

Adam said, "Bruce, I know your heart and what you desire for others. I know you want them to feel loved. I didn't feel loved as I read it."

He knew it was a book about Jesus' love and he wanted to open the book and be swept up in that love. And not as an emotional response, although that does sell, but from a place of being drawn into the wider reality of what love is intended to look like in Christian community. He expected to form a connection with me at the onset so that he would want to journey with me through the rest of the book. So that's what I'd like to do, invite you to join me as I explore what it means to live out Jesus' New Command. So let's start at the beginning.

SHRUGS NOT HUGS

From as far back as I can remember, until the age of ten, my family was always pretty affectionate. I come from a big Italian family, so we were always together, and I remember a lot of physical affection. Beyond the random adult ruffling your hair as you walked past, there were moments like climbing into my grandpa's (Poppy) bed and asking him to tell us a story. He'd lay there with his arm around as many of us kids that could fit and tell us wonderful stories about his life. He was tough; fingernails dug into our scalp when we misbehaved kind of tough, but he was often soft-spoken and gentle. He equalized and even quieted the noise in my family. I also remember my Aunt Jo being a kisser. As a kid, she would chase you around, sweep you up and plant huge kisses on your face. Then she'd make you dance with her. She loved to dance. Barry Manilow was her poison. And then, there was of course my grandma. She was the quintessential Old Italian Lady. She was always concerned about whether you'd eaten. You never stepped inside her house without giving her a hug and kiss. She always told me that as a baby, I cried all the time. She even called me a "baby cry," but she always doted over me. I was her youngest son's first baby, and he was her baby, so I think that mattered to her. There was always love. Always. At the time I wouldn't have known how to qualify it, but now I look at all of those little things, the stories, the dancing, the "baby cry," and know that all of that was how I knew I was theirs. I belonged to them.

My Poppy passed away in April 1987. Even though I was only 10 years old, it didn't take long for me to realize that he was the glue that held everything together. There was tension in my family and my Poppy was the one who bridged that gap and held it at bay. Shortly after he passed the conflict in our family became too much. As a result, we moved away from southern California to Anchorage, Alaska. After our move things weren't the same in my family. Part of that might have been the stark difference between the beaches and city-life of southern California and the snow and wilderness of the Last Frontier, but life had changed. Both my parents worked a lot to make ends meet. If my mom wasn't working, then my dad worked doubly hard. All in all, things were extremely hard.

At the end of our first year in Alaska, when I was 12 years old, I became the victim of a violent crime. It was in the wake of that event, and through the invitation of my dad's boss, that my family became Christians. My conversion to Christianity only created confusion in me because I already considered myself "damaged and broken." Being violated and becoming a victim destroyed my ability to trust anyone, even God. Asking me to believe that I was loved and could find wholeness and healing was too much to ask me to expect. If I think back, that was the point at which I think I started living a life focused on striving, even if I didn't know what I was striving for. At the least I wanted my heart and mind healed from the hurt I had experienced and somehow it always eluded me. It just felt like everyone shrugged it off, as if to say, "Eh, there's not much I can do for you. Good luck." Feeling like no one was able to help me was awful. I heard the good things the pastor preached about God, even though it was often wrapped in a message about needing to be good, and I wanted Him so badly. But I was already hurt and broken, so the way my 12-year-old mind internalized that was to believe that I couldn't be good enough. That hurt and brokenness would impact the way I understood and handled relationships through the next 20 years.

ATTABOY

In August 2019 one of my friends preached a sermon about how he grew up in a very performance-based environment. He worked hard and long, ensuring excellence was the main staple of that work, hoping for a pat on the back and to hear the words, "Attaboy! Good job!" It was his drug of choice. He went on to make the point about the many people, especially men, who base their self-worth and value on other people's acknowledgement of their accomplishments. It's a performance-based reward system. Essentially, your worth, and often identity, is built on people acknowledging that your work is good, thus, you must be good. While acknowledging someone's good work is important, the problem with it being the ultimate standard is when the work isn't good or if it goes unacknowledged, then the person doing the work isn't good and/or becomes unimportant.

As he preached, I came to the realization, which I think I already knew on a lot of different levels, that my performance was not about acknowledging how good of a job I did. Instead mine was appreciation-based. I didn't have an *"attaboy"* problem; I had a *"that's my boy"* one. I wasn't looking for acknowledgement of how good a job I did or even to please others through my work; I was looking to belong to someone through an expression of love. With my acts of service, I wanted to please others into them loving me. I know now that it was attempting to manipulate the situation in a way that put me in the best position for me to receive love.

As I approached my teenage years, the ability to manipulate manifested in my ability to become a chameleon. I learned how to fit into almost any environment or group by looking at what they valued in their group members. Even though I didn't play sports, I hung with the jocks because I could talk my way through the topics and knew what boosted their egos. I didn't play an instrument, but the band geeks were easy friends because I liked music and knew how to flatter them for their skills. The stoners, preppies, techies (known then as A/V nerds, mostly just Walkmans and VHS players), Christian school kids (they were some of the worst and most fun), JROTC (Junior Reserve Officer Training Corps), and the emo kids were all "my" people. There was even a stint when I was 16 that I was a part of a party crew, which was primarily made up of Hispanic members in SoCal. I'm not joking. I went by the name, "lil'Boink" because the leader went by "Boink" and I wanted him to like me. Everything I did was focused on getting people to like me, because if they liked me, maybe that meant that they loved me. And if they loved me, maybe then I would belong somewhere.

By the time I was 18 years old I had already had a bunch of shallow relationships. I had engaged in drinking and drugs, multiple sexual encounters, and left home by my 18th birthday. All of my striving for connection, all of the destructive behavior, and all of the looking for *my people* had failed to meet my need for belonging. I viewed every intimate relationship with a girl as an opportunity to feel loved and as proof that maybe I was lovable, if even just a little. Because I was always focused on what *I* needed, any time that I suspected that the relationship was about to end, often without any credible proof, I ended it first. Rejecting was always safer than being rejected. By rejecting them, it was easier to convince myself that my lack of feeling loved was because of something they were or weren't doing. At the same time, I used every encounter with drugs and alcohol as an opportunity for acceptance or as one to numb the pain. All relationships, all people, and all interactions were simply methods to meet my need to feel loved. It would take a long time for me to realize how much I manipulated people and situations because I didn't feel loved, and ultimately how detrimental it would be to my understanding of love and God.

CRASHING INTO HOPE

To say that life between 18 and 32 was eventful would be a gross understatement. I joined the U.S. Air Force as a police officer. I quickly got married. Ultimately it was a marriage of convenience; we both needed something and the other seemed to provide it. I think she needed to be saved from certain aspects of life and since I fancied myself the saving kind, I accepted the role. It worked for a while; not well, but enough that it lasted for 12 years. I also had two sons, moved with the military four times, almost got divorced, deployed in the wake of the terror attacks on September 11, 2001, taught at the Air Force Police Academy, and earned my master's degree. I also drank and partied *a lot* and I had an extra-marital affair. I don't mean to throw those last two in there like they aren't serious; they were and are, but at the time they were a part of that searching. I was lost and issues in my marriage that I didn't know how to handle only made it more difficult to parse out what love was supposed to look and feel like. I had convinced myself, even while going to church and being a "Christian" that those activities were acceptable because "we all deserve to be loved" and I had yet to find it. Marriage and children weren't an antidote to not feeling loved. In fact, because I didn't know what it was supposed to feel like to be loved, I often felt like I was failing my wife and children in that area.

It all came crashing down on that night in September, 2008. Drugs, drinking, marriage, success at work, affairs, friendships, and even Christianity had failed to satisfy my need for love and belonging. By the time that my ex-wife had left, I hated the idea of love. I had convinced myself that it wasn't meant for everyone. Maybe love was reserved for a select and deserving few; maybe those were the *elect* that I had heard some in the church speak about. When I made that declaration of my separation from God, I had fully intended to leave Christianity. I still believed that He existed, but I didn't believe that He cared. In hindsight, it seems worse to believe that God doesn't care than believing that He doesn't exist. Regardless, I had never experienced the loving Father that some purported God to be. I certainly hadn't been able to see or delineate His involvement in my life. How could all of this have happened if I had been practicing the Christianity I had been taught? How could this happen if I mattered to Him? I couldn't have been farther from understanding John's declaration, "God is love."[1]

That night, that I declared being done, almost as if God was answering my questions, my 9-year-old son walked into the room and asked me if we could go back to the church that we had visited a couple weeks prior. I weighed my responses and immediately knew I didn't want to be responsible for my son not knowing God. He needed to make his own decision about the type of Father that God was, so I agreed we'd go back. The Sunday that we went back, pastor Jeff Maness, who would later become my friend and mentor, said he felt like God directed him to break from the sermon he had prepared and share with others that there is certainty in an uncertain world. The crux of the message was that regardless of what circumstances occur in our life, no matter how uncertain things look, Jesus is a constant and the only certainty. During the entirety of the service I knew God was directing it at me. For the first time I felt like God saw me. In a moment my Christianity crashed into hope.

THEY WERE HIS

After I left the church service I went home, went straight to my bedroom, and cried and prayed. Well, if you consider yelling at God praying, then I was praying really hard. I couldn't understand why if everything the pastor said about Jesus was true, that He was loving, full of grace and mercy, our steadfast rock, the only thing that was certain, even and especially through uncertainty, of which I had overflowing amounts, then how come I had never experienced it? In twenty years of Christianity I had never experienced Jesus in the way he described. I had only ever experienced Father God as judgmental and disapproving, full of wrath and anger. Why had no one ever explained Jesus that way? And, why was this pastor the one who gets to say he sees it correctly? I probably cried and "prayed" for a solid hour. During that time, I got stuck on asking God, "Why did you leave? Why did you reject me like everyone else? Why wasn't I good enough?" At the end of the hour I found myself sitting on the end of the bed, both physically and emotionally exhausted. As I sat there, I felt God say, not in an audible voice, but in a sensation that filled my whole body, "I never left you. It was you who never showed your face to Me." In 20 years I had never felt God's presence like that, and I had certainly never felt like He had answered any of my prayers. His answer wasn't that I hadn't behaved according to His standard. It was that I had never made myself available to Him. I was undone and knew I couldn't simply walk away.

When I was growing up I had heard the words "God is love." Pastors preached on it, it was on bumper stickers, and might have even been painted on my youth room wall at the church. I also knew we were supposed to love God with all our heart, soul, mind, and strength, and love our neighbor as ourselves. There seemed to be no shortage of sermons on love, but they were primarily focused on loving God and our neighbor. My problem was that I never understood it. What I saw in the churches I attended was a lack of what I assumed love was meant to look like. It played itself out in families, who surely loved each other, but you knew things weren't okay and no one walked with them in it. It was Sunday morning hand shakes between people who were barely holding it together, but they mustered the ability to paint on smiles and give the traditional "busy" response when asked how they were doing. It didn't seem loving and as far as I was concerned, if I could get the same "love" in the world without God's rule, which I often felt were unreasonable, then why wouldn't I choose the world?

I rarely, if ever, heard that we were supposed to love each other. Maybe I knew it was a command in the Bible, but I honestly can't remember ever hearing it from any Christian that I knew, not even a pastor. Our lack of knowing and teaching about loving each other is the reason Gaylord Enns, in his book *Love Revolution*, calls it the "forgotten command." If you look at the material being put out by many western Christian churches, and even many of the church forefathers, the New Command, to "love one another as [Christ] has loved you" is not a predominant theme. I might go as far as to say it isn't even a sub-theme. But if we read Jesus' words in John 13, it's supposed to be THE theme of what it means to follow Jesus and be citizens of His New Covenant. What I heard on that Sunday was different.

I kept going to that church and over the next couple months I began to see Jesus differently. He was becoming my Savior in all things. I still didn't get or feel the love thing, but at least I felt like He was present and inviting me to walk with Him. Eventually I emailed Jeff to share what God had been showing me. That email would be the start of a friendship and four years of counseling and coaching that would let me see and experience God like never before. Jesus wasn't peripheral anymore. I wanted to know Him, walk with Him, and love Him; I just didn't know how. Part of my email to Jeff dealt with my long time feeling that God had been calling me to ministry. All of the things I used as excuses had been removed; so I wanted to see what it would look like to embrace that call. Ultimately that curiosity would find me helping in our church's college/young adult ministry, theSHIFT. Because my transition from teen to adult was so turbulent, I thought I might be able to help other young adults make smoother ones. In reality, they would help me transition into my spiritual adulthood instead.

From my very first interactions with theSHIFT community I knew they were different. Almost immediately I saw the type of love that I had been hearing about for the past 6 months. I didn't recognize it as love at first, but it was different than anything I had ever seen. I often tell people that they were so good and at the same time, so bad at relationships, but it always worked because they wanted Jesus and tried hard to default to love. Even when they were angry with one another and it seemed like there was no hope of forgiveness, love often won out. Of course there were some, who would leave, but for the majority of that small group, they wanted Jesus and for them, that included each other. In fact, they wanted Him so badly that they understood, at least on the most basic level, that you couldn't have Him without accepting each other as His bride. They had learned that it's a package deal.

When I first started spending time with them I couldn't put my finger on what was different about their love compared to other church settings I'd experienced. They claimed to love God and love people, which were meant to point to the Great Commandment. Of course it's biblical, but in the past I had seen it take the form of community outreach (love people) and streamlined and showy Sunday services (love God). Loving God and loving people make for a great mission statement, but just plastering it on your church walls doesn't mean you do it well. In 20 years as a Christian, I had never experienced that command done well and now, somehow, these young adults had figured it out? There was something inside their group that drove their ability to love in a way that revealed them as genuine lovers of God and people. And it wasn't just in their weekly gatherings or in the service projects they did. It was a love that radiated from them and all their activities were a byproduct of it.

A lot of that can be attributed to the people who were leading theSHIFT at the time, Curtis and Heather Marshall. It was their understanding of Jesus' love and their willingness to try, and sometimes fail, at applying that love in real life that made theSHIFT different. One of the things they understood was that it takes time to build relationships, so they built theSHIFT with the expectation. They dedicated themselves and the group to time with God, time with His Word, and time with each other. Because they knew it would take time, they committed to being in it for the long haul. Curt and Heather also understood that our relationship with Jesus was critically dependent on our relationship with Jesus' Body and vice versa. It was evident to me that they understood and tried to live out the Apostle John's declaration that you cannot love God if you do not love your brother and sister in Christ.[2] It was the love that they had for one another that made it clear that they belonged to Him and to each other; and I wanted the same thing.

I had spent 20 years as a Christian before I came across a group who was trying to figure out what it meant to live out the New Command, to love each other; even if they didn't know that was the command they were practicing. The years I spent with theSHIFT ruined me for church, but it ruined me in the most glorious way possible. Because of my time with that community, I could no longer simply attend church on Sunday mornings. Tithing without doing was no longer an option. I couldn't sit back and watch my Christian brothers and sisters suffer, whether it was financially, health-wise, relationally, or spiritually, and be okay with the multiple outreach projects being directed to a world outside of Jesus' bride. At the time that I left theSHIFT, I hadn't yet realized that they were practicing the New Command, that realization came years later, but I knew they were doing something different, and it was good. By the time the military moved us to Japan and away from that community, I was different, and I saw the Church differently.

FROM THERE TO HERE

I love God's church. I took the long way around in this journey toward the New Command, but God is faithful to complete the work He starts.[3] There was a time that I was convinced that the church was "doing it wrong" and that my friends and I had figured out the better way. God corrected my heart and showed me that it wasn't about a model, but rather, a mindset. As God walked me through my journey, I started focusing on this idea of community. There are a lot of pastors and church leaders, especially more recently, who have recognized the lack of connectedness within the body and have started the process of trying to figure out what it looks like to be in community with other believers. Unfortunately, that process, for a lot of reasons, but largely because of the business of doing church, often causes community to become a program, primarily because programs are how we quantify achievement. We are able to put instruments in place for collecting metrics and measuring success. When the numbers don't add up to what we've marked as successful, we change the program. When we do that, we turn community that is intended to be one of our vehicles for discipleship into another event we attend so that we can check off the discipleship box. To be clear, small group communities are beneficial. I grew in my knowledge of God in them, but knowledge that isn't transformed into action is useless in the Kingdom. I was seeing too many people who attended Sunday service and weekly small groups still feel and live disconnected from the body. They were the same people who were struggling in their faith, burning out from "over serving" at and in church, and secretly struggling to believe and trust that God was a good Father who loved them. For too long I had been one of those people and theSHIFT helped me see something differently. I saw Jesus differently. I saw His bride differently. I saw them joined spectacularly together and it was beautiful. It was the way it was meant to be and it changed everything. So I set out trying to figure out how to develop and be a part of a community that practiced Jesus' command to love one another.

The answer seemed to be wrapped up in the amount and purpose of the time that Christians spent together. I started looking at what elements of community created connectedness within the body and ultimately between Jesus and His Bride. My motivation quickly became very much about reforming the model for how we've come to "do" church. I would often tell people that we (my friends and I) hadn't figured out *the* way to do church, just a way, but in my heart I knew I believed that I had figured out a better way, the right way. I became more and more convinced that I had figured out the elements that created connection and genuine community. As I think back, I know that the process I went through trying to figure out a better way to do church was built out of the lack of connection and the very real hurt and rejection that I had experienced for most of my life. I was trying to give form to a concept that promoted connectedness and belonging in a real, Heaven-come-to-earth-now, way. I always tried to make sure that at the center of it was Jesus bringing His Good News; after all, it's about Him. The concept and process itself was biblical, almost all of it being built out of Acts 2:42-27. But I always felt like there was something missing; and not something small, but something significant.

SOUP FOR YOU! WELL, CHILI.

One evening, during my time leading theSHIFT, there was a knock on my door. I had just gotten home from work and I think was still in my uniform. It was a Thursday night and my sons and I were about to start family night. I opened the door and there stood one of my SHIFT people holding a crockpot. I said hi and asked her what was going on. She told me that she and some of the other members had decided they would start cooking dinner for my sons and me on Thursdays so we could focus on family night. Then she handed me the crockpot, said she loved us, and left. As I closed the door I felt a few tears escape from my eyes. I stood there holding our dinner trying to figure out what I was feeling. It took a few minutes, but I finally realized it was love. I felt loved. And not just love. It was, "Jesus love." In fact, it was the first time that I remember feeling, in 20 years, the literal and tangible love of Jesus. I was loved. That day, Jesus stood at my door and declared His love for me by dropping off soup, although, now that I think about it, it may have been chili.

Some years later, I was reflecting on my Jesus chili and the scripture about loving one another popped in my head. Clearly, it was God who drew it all together for me, but nonetheless, it had become glaringly obvious. The time spent together, the grace for and forgiveness of one another, service to each other, seeking God together, submitting to one another, all of their gatherings, their desire to grow in Christ and invite others in, and yes, the dinner too, were all aspects of theSHIFT members learning to obey Jesus' New Command to love each other as He had loved them. I saw the Gospel, Jesus' sacrifice, in the way my people were practicing the New Command. That was the missing piece: the New Command.

JOIN ME

I built my life on serving others: in the military, law enforcement, and church. Most of it was wrongly motivated. Sometimes it was for acceptance, and sometimes so I would look good. Most of the time it was geared toward getting something in return. Service, especially in Christianity, is never intended to be like that. It certainly isn't intended to be done out of some false sense of obligation or as a means to experience the love of God. On the contrary, it is intended to originate from a place of knowing love so fully that you can't help but serve others as an expression of that love, and in doing so, invite them into the knowledge of that same love. When I finally realized all of this and that it was the New Command that differentiated us from the world and even those bound to the Old Covenant, everything changed.

The intent of this book is not to undermine the two thousand years of teaching and the thousands of writings by church fathers and theologians, who are undoubtedly smarter than I am. Instead, it is intended to echo Enns's call to recover this New Command, which Jesus intentionally separates from the other two commands of the Old Covenant. I'm confident that obedience to this command is the key to us being an active part of the fulfillment of the Old Covenant, so that we can live freely in the New Covenant.

This is my love letter to Jesus' Bride. This is the culmination of an almost 7-year writing journey of discovering what it means to live as a New Covenant citizen of Heaven. This book is also my invitation for you to join me in the discovery of what it means to love each other, love God, and love your neighbor. I no longer want or even care about how churches "do" church. All I care about is why they do it. Sunday morning is meant to be one thing we do and should be a time of glad celebration and communal worship. It is a time that the saints of God can gather in one place to learn and be edified and sometimes admonished by the living word of God. It should be about coming together as a collective body and remembering Jesus as our head and the mission He has placed in our hearts. The events of Sunday should a culmination of a week spent gathering with other Christians, seeking God together, and learning mutual submission through the practice of loving one another, the way that Jesus loves us, so that we might be moved toward a life of sacrifice focused on inviting our neighbors into the Kingdom.

When we gather we should be asking ourselves: Are we focused on placing Jesus at the center, recognizing that He is among us, like He promised, and that He is teaching us to love each other? I want to help other Christians understand that practicing the command to love each other is our act of loving God, because Jesus said that obeying His commands is how we show our love for Him. Since He is one with the Father, and God the Son, loving each other becomes our first act of loving God. When we understand what it means to love God and start living in that truth, we are compelled toward serving and loving our neighbors in a way that invites them into the Good King's Kingdom.

This book is not about some wishy-washy kind of love. This book is about a love, commanded by Jesus, which compels us as followers, in every action toward our brothers and sisters in Him. It's about a kind of love that ought to be commonly practiced by His bride and which fulfills the old law, reveals our love for God, and compels us to love our neighbors for the purpose of revealing Jesus to them. It isn't a purposeless love. It's a love that reveals truth and transforms us into the very likeness of Him who laid down His life for us, His friends. It's about a love that tells the rest of the world that we are His. It's about a simple kind of love that isn't always easy to extend. Nothing that is really good is ever very easy. What is easy is becoming stuck in the Old Covenant way of thinking. We've been stuck there for millennia. It's easy to get stuck on Jesus' declaration of the two Greatest Commands of the Old Covenant and miss that He said He came to fulfill it. He started that well before His work on the cross and that is what we're going to work through in this book.

I wrote this book because I want to help the body understand the importance, seriousness, and joy connected to and received from following Jesus' New Command. Second only to our belief in Jesus, the New Command is the crux of the New Covenant and the way that we experience Jesus' fulfillment of the Law. I'm writing this book because I believe Jesus when He said that the world would believe that we are His and that God sent Him when we are unified in our love for each other. I want the church to learn what it means to live as Kingdom citizens who are committed to practicing the kind of love defined in 1 Corinthians 13. This is how we experience God's Law fulfilled. When we experience God's Law fulfilled, we experience life more abundant; life exceedingly above what we would know outside of His love. When you experience the love of Jesus, through the New Command, it changes everything. You are no longer able to be content with just showing up on Sunday mornings to hear good music and a good moral message. All of the sudden you are compelled to be with other Christians, a lot. And Sunday's gathering becomes a weekly culminating celebration of the goodness of God. It moves you toward a better understanding of what Jesus meant when He talked about things like mercy, serving, compassion, hope, and faith. And all of that happens in the midst of finding and being with your people and experiencing a love unlike any other. Among the body you find a love that accepts you as you are, but transforms you into His likeness. Will you join me?

Part One

WHAT IS LOVE?

WHENEVER I HEAR THAT QUESTION, I immediately initiate the required Night at the Roxbury side head-bob courtesy of Haddaway's 1993 chart-topper by the same name. After that's taken care of, I would generally answer, "It's an action." You probably think that's the most cliché answer possible. It is, but it's still true. I do believe that genuine love looks like a decision to meet others' needs. But, over the last few years, God has been expanding my understanding of what love is and how He intended it to play out in Christian community. If you asked me today, I would say that I'm convinced love is a person who prompts us to meet others' needs.

In order to get there, I had to wrestle with believing that God is actually Love. In the same way, truth is in and is Jesus; love is in and is God. And because "love is a person" is critical to this whole love idea, we have to have that as our starting place for talking about Jesus fulfilling the law through love, with His New Command.

While it's true that we too quickly go to cliché answers about love, what's also true is we've over-simplified the answer so much that it has almost lost any deep meaning. In fact, I think we've almost stopped putting thought into what real love is because we handle it so flippantly. We effortlessly toss the word love around without any regard for the depth of its seriousness. And it is serious. So serious that it has been the premise used for starting entire religions and some of the most significant world-changing events. And unfortunately, it has also been the source of some of the most heinous crimes.

And if it wasn't already serious enough, as Christians, love takes on an even heavier weight. For us, love is so significant that depending on the translation of the Bible you're reading, it appears anywhere from 310 to 538 times. The idea of love even makes it into our church rhetoric, evidenced by constant recitation and use in church mottos. Love God and love people. It's a noble call and biblical, at that. Sadly, because we don't really understand what that means, we often do it poorly, if at all. To love God and others well, we must understand what love is; and not in some all-encompassing "I love pizza" sort of way, but in a more profound biblical way that allows for more meaningful application. Learning what it means to say God is Love enables us to love in a more real way. Only after gaining that understanding can we recognize the shortcomings in substituting the law for loving God and others. This is the foundation for what it means to be loved and give love. As we lay this foundation, I encourage you to pause often and use the Bible to reflect along the way.

1

GOD IS LOVE

The one who does not love does not know God, because God is love.
~ 1 John 4:8 ~

IF YOU'RE A CHRISTIAN, then you've heard God is love. John says it in the Bible; we listen to it preached on Sunday mornings, and we say it repeatedly. It's ingrained in us from the moment we're saved and infused into our language. We put it on bumper stickers and bracelets. We know the words "God is love," but do we know what it means when we say it?

In the scripture above, "God is love" wasn't some flippant piece of information attached to admonish unloving people. On the contrary, this was a definitive statement about the very essence of God and how we, His children, are intended to reflect it. This verse was the Holy Spirit's revelation, through John, about our God. John did not say, "God loves," is "like love," or "is loving," he said, "God is love." You could almost capitalize "Love" in this instance because John seems to be using it as a synonym for God. So, what does he mean? What was John telling us about God?

"God is love" is a verse that's easy to breeze over and miss the depth of its importance. Read it again.

God is love.
He IS love.

John is revealing a vital piece of information about God the Father. He is telling us that the very core, the identifying nature, of who God is and the thing that separates Him from gods of other religions, is that He is the very expression of how we ought to interpret and define love. Unfortunately, humans have a knack for defining things in ways that satisfy our needs.

LOVE AS AN IDOL

Among some theologians, one of the main concerns regarding the "God is love" scripture is our propensity to make things idols. In this case, the fear is that if we equate love with God, we run the risk of making love our ultimate desire and the thing we worship rather than worshiping God. In one of his sermons, pastor and author, A.W. Tozer, said this of the verse:

> Equating love with God is a major mistake that has produced much unsound religious philosophy and has brought forth a spate of vaporous poetry completely out of accord with the Holy Scriptures and altogether of another climate from that of historic Christianity. Had the apostle declared that love is what God is, we would be forced to infer that God is what love is. If literally God is love, then literally love is God, and we are in all duty-bound to worship love as the only God there is. If love is equal to God then God is only equal to love, and God and love are identical. Thus we destroy the concept of personality in God and deny outright all His attributes save one, and that one we substitute for God.

I respect and agree with Tozer on a lot of things. His writings and sermons are among some of the very best and quite ahead of their time. His book, *The Pursuit of God*, will indiscriminately wreck anyone who opens it. It is not my intention to challenge Tozer's work, only his interpretation of the apostle's declaration. But, I cannot do that without first admitting that there is some very real validity to his concern. We do tend to worship other things apart from and/or in place of God. If that were not the case, God wouldn't have needed to include it as a commandment, Do not have other gods besides Me. In this way, Tozer's fear is rightly justified.

The 19th Century Indian author, Rabindranath Tagore, said, "Love is the only reality and it is not a mere sentiment. It is the ultimate truth that lies at the heart of creation." Deepak Chopra, author and New Age movement teacher, reiterated that sentiment by proclaiming, "Love is the ultimate truth at the heart of the universe and transcends all boundaries." I even found a reference to Michael Jackson saying, "Let us dream of tomorrow where we can truly love from the soul, and know love as the ultimate truth at the heart of all creation." All of these thinkers have had substantial influence in our culture and have communicated the very intentional message, "love is the ultimate truth." And while that seems noble, it makes the pursuit of love the most crucial thing, rather than the pursuit of the one who is Love. In doing so, they have done the very thing that Tozer warns against. This view elevates love to god-like status and makes it this ethereal substance that seems just out of our reach; as if it is something that we should strive for beyond all else, but that is ultimately unattainable and indefinable. The good news is it's not.

When we take a closer look at this view of love as a pursuit, it becomes apparent that it is a response to the human need to find meaning. As I've read and researched, I discovered that a central tenant in the New Age doctrine places divinity on humanity as co-creators. There's a lot of talk about reuniting with "god," but no real explanation of who or what "god" is. Because of that lack of definition, it makes sense that love would take an elevated seat and become the thing at the center of creation, the object that we ought to pursue above all else. Unfortunately, there's no real definition of that either. And because one of the other main focuses of New Age-ism is "feel goodism" (meaning do what you like, as long as it doesn't hurt anyone else), the pursuit of the "only real reality," love, becomes a selfish one. This is the view of love that we see threaded throughout our culture.

You don't need to look far to see selfishness as the primary motive for pursuing love. Humans have made an art form out of ending relationships because; "I'm just not in love with them anymore." What we actually mean is, "I don't feel the same butterflies as I did when we first fell in love, and I'm not wasting my time on this." This is also why extramarital affairs, dating multiple people at the same time, and the "hook-up" culture have become the norm in our current society. For any number of reasons, we decide that one person is no longer worthy of our love and someone else is. WE get to be the one who defines love. One deeper issue connected to that misapplication and misunderstanding of love is that we've placed love and lust on equal ground.

In many cases, not just on equal ground, but we've confused lust for love. To be fair, apart from God, that's not a far leap to make. Many of the feelings and brain chemistry are the same when it comes to lust and love. When love becomes separated from the person of God and turned into an ethereal substance that is the focus of our primary pursuit, anything goes. Without real definition, love becomes anything that makes us feel good. This was the danger Tozer was talking about when we place love as the center of our focus.

In that regard, not only does it become our highest purpose, but it also becomes the measuring stick for declaring our affinity for nearly anything we enjoy. We love our spouse, but at the same time, we love a good steak. We love our sports team, our dog, chocolate, skiing, and a good book. If we enjoy it, then we love it. We've misunderstood and misused the word love so much that we've minimized it to a word without substance. Most often we say those things without meaning to minimize it, but we do. By elevating love to the place of ultimate truth, we begin to worship it, and Tozer's fear becomes real. And because humans have a penchant for control, even to control that which we worship, we wrestle love to the ground, subdue it and force it to mean what we want it to mean. In doing so, we separate it from the divine and cast it among the common.

LOVE AS A VERB

In my first marriage, I wasn't very concerned with being in a relationship with God. Jesus might have been my Savior, but as I mentioned, He was peripheral and would primarily be the one who would judge me based on my behavior. I had held that view for almost a decade before I was married. Because of that, I had a pretty warped understanding of love. For me, love was nothing more than a feeling. I know that this gets into a more significant discussion, and I still believe that there is a "love" feeling, or more accurately, a collection of feelings, but at the time, love was just a feeling that came and went. And because my view of love was very selfish, in my marriage it was gone more than it was there. When it was gone, there was little I could do if I wasn't "feeling it." For a lot of people, that's how they "fall out of love."

Misunderstanding love as a feeling, coupled with our culture and our church continually telling me, "love is a verb," I, like a lot of married people, was set up to fail. It wasn't that love being a verb was intrinsically a bad thing, it isn't, and I'll explain that more in a second, but when we detach it from something more profound, it can become as shallow an action as turning a light on or off.

For me, love became the thing I was obligated to do inside of my marriage, whether I felt anything or not because "good" Christians don't get divorced. With that mindset, loving my ex-wife became about doing the "right" things to make sure we stayed married; because how would I look to other Christians if I couldn't make my marriage work? So I did my part and she did hers. We stayed and did our duty to "love" one another. My obligation to "love" her, as a husband, took the form of doing all my chores, buying her stuff – it was one of my main substitutions for having to love her, saying right things, and hiding my "mess-ups" as best as I could. During that time in our marriage, if you had asked me if I loved her, I would have answered "yes" without a second thought because everything I did proved it. And even though it looked like we were doing our best to love each other, we were just operating out of selfishness.

That is the danger in disconnecting love from the divine and making it purely a human decision and action. When we do this, it becomes more about us than anyone else. To be fair, it usually isn't done intentionally; it just happens that way. We're self-focused creatures. When love becomes an ultimate goal and becomes a purely decision-based activity, we will always bend it toward fulfilling our needs first.

Today I know I wasn't doing it so that she would know I loved her or even so that she would feel loved. When I look back now, because I understand love a little better, I was doing it to make sure I received love. The understanding of love that I had was a quid pro quo one. I thought that if I decided to do the things that looked like I loved her, I could provoke her to behave in a way that was "loving" toward me. When she stopped being loving, I had permission to stop and vice versa. I know that this sounds like a perspective thing, and it is. But what I'm arguing is that this has become our standard view of love as an action. Our decision to act in loving ways is often centered on reciprocity and is a result of separating it from something deeper.

Dick Foth is an author, former pastor, and former university president. When I lived in the Washington D.C. metro area, I attended National Community Church, where he preached often. His sermons were always fantastic, so filled with wisdom and evident love for God and the people he shepherded. During one particular sermon about loving others, he defined love as "the accurate estimate and the adequate supply of another person's need." When I heard him say it I knew it was right. It was a far better way of defining love than, "love is a verb." It still communicates love as an action, but in defining it this way he adds a depth to it that meaningfully shifts the focus to the person being loved. It's almost a perfect definition. I would only add two small words: without expectation. Love is the accurate estimate and adequate supply of another person's need, without expectation. So love is a verb. But, it isn't just a verb; it's also a noun.

LOVE AS THE ESSENCE OF GOD

One of Tozer's main concerns, apart from making love into something we worship, was that we might dismiss all of God's other characteristics, sans one. If we want to see God rightly and be submitted to Him through the truth of scripture, we have to acknowledge what it says about Him. Isaiah

30:18 says, "For the LORD is a God of justice." Nahum 12:2 says, "The Lord is a jealous and avenging God; the Lord is avenging and wrathful." In one verse we get both jealousy and wrath. So what do we do with those truths? The thing is, while all that scripture is true, the Bible doesn't say that God is those characteristics in the same way it says He is love. Yes, God is a jealous God, but He isn't jealousy. He is wrathful, but not wrath. He's just, but not justice. There is a clear distinction between what He is and what He's like; it's a matter of *essence* and *identity*.

In 1871 bible commentators, Robert Jamieson, A. R. Fausset and David Brown said this in their commentary on 1 John 4:8:

> There is no Greek article to love, but to God; therefore, we cannot translate, Love is God. **GOD IS** fundamentally and essentially **LOVE: NOT MERELY IS LOVING**, for then John's argument would not stand; for the conclusion from the premises then would be this, This man is not loving: God is loving; therefore he knoweth not God in so far as God is loving; still he might know Him in His other attributes. But when we take love as God's essence, the argument is sound: This man doth not love, and therefore knows not love: **GOD IS ESSENTIALLY LOVE**, therefore he knows not God. (emphasis added)

From the outset, it is easy to confuse essence and identity as similar things. They both have to do with what makes up a person. The easiest way to present them is by the definitions.

Identity: the distinguishing character or personality of an individual.

Essence: the intrinsic nature or indispensable quality of something, especially something abstract, that determines its character.

For the word *essence*, several other definitions make the point more explicit. For example, "the basic, real, and invariable nature of a thing or its significant individual feature or features." Another says, "the most significant element, quality, or aspect of a thing or person." But I think my favorite is the one used to define it in the sphere of philosophy. That definition is "a property or group of properties of something without which it would not exist or be what it is." All that to say, this: when it comes to God, *essence* and *identity*, while related, identify distinct aspects of Him.

Identity is an important word in our culture. Most of us can take someone questioning our actions, as long as they're not ascribed as part of who we are. For example, if I'm not usually an "angry person," but I get really angry at a particular situation or person and respond in a way that I typically wouldn't, people can dismiss it as me "acting out of character." And, because I know that isn't the type of person I am, and don't consider it as a part of my identity, I'm okay with someone telling me that I probably overreacted. Maybe not while I'm angry, but eventually I'd be okay with it. But, if I determine a specific characteristic is a part of who I am, then it becomes, "I can't change that! It's just who I am."

For better or worse, we hold tightly to those things we associate with who we are as a person. That's why conversations involving our identity can be so tricky. It's one of the main reasons why we have such difficulty believing who God says we are. We tend to attach what we do to who we are. It's also one of the main reasons we introduce ourselves by our occupation and why we make excuses for being too cynical, or angry, or even too happy. We like to use the excuse "that's just who I am" because it's easier than the alternative that it might be a character trait that isn't actually a part of who we are.
We opt for believing we are unlovable rather than realizing that we've been unloved. It's also the reason why conversation like the one surrounding homosexuality is such a volatile one. Right or wrong, Christians view it from a behavioral point-of-view; while someone who is gay views it as identity. While I'm not going to get into that distinction, it does demonstrate the weight and impact that identity has on us as individuals and within our culture.

This same weight applies to God's identity. Part of the purpose of the Bible is God revealing Himself (what He's like, how He acts, who He is) to us, so we are better able to recognize Him. One of the main reasons that God gave us this revelation is to make known those character traits that set Him apart from the other gods that people were worshiping at that time. God wanted us to know, as fully as humanly possible, who He is, and that involves His defining characteristics or His identity. But that is separate from the core of who He is; that is His essence.

Essence is something altogether more profound. As the definition explains, it is the intrinsic, or fundamental, nature of something and is the thing that determines its character. It also says this especially applies to abstract ideas. Quick side note: God the Father, while legitimately possessing personhood,

He created it and we see it manifested in Adam and later, more perfectly in Christ, He is ultimately intangible, technically giving Him an abstract quality.

In this instance, whatever God's fundamental nature is will determine His characteristics and how they play out in His personality and toward us. So then what is His essence, His fundamental nature? John answers that question by telling us that God is Love.

Love is the abstract substance that makes up the most basic and essential core of who God is, and you cannot separate Him from it. Nor can love be separated from Him, lest He ceases being God. It is love that determines, defines and directs His character. That means instead of jealousy, we get selfless jealousy. And instead of anger, we get righteous anger, divine justice, rather than justice, and a just wrath, instead of wrath for wrath's sake. It is He, as Love, who informs all His other characteristics. He doesn't simply love, He is love, and because of that, He cannot respond any other way, except out of love. This is good news for us because His essence is what assures His unchanging goodness toward us. His love is not merely a chemical reaction in His brain that causes Him to feel affection for us. It is deeper seated and more real than that. Our confusion about and mishandling of what love is and what "God is Love" means, does not undo the truth of scripture or who He is.

LOVE SPELLED G-O-D

Maybe one of the reasons that love is mentioned so much in the Bible, 424-ish times depending on the translation you use, is because it's important to God. Jesus said, "Just as I have loved you, you must also love one another." If we are going to love the way Jesus has commanded us, then we need to have a better understanding of love as essence. One way we can start to love like Jesus is by understanding that not only is love the thing that determines God's characteristics, but it is also what drives His actions.

Love is the reason that He created the earth. Genesis tells us that we're created in His image,[1] Isaiah says that the earth is filled with His glory,[2] and Jesus connects the two by declaring God's glory is that we would bear much fruit, showing ourselves to be His disciples.[3] If God's essence is love, then by creating us in His image, He has imbued us with the same essence as a means of showcasing His glory in all the earth. And we reflect that glory by bearing forth much fruit, which Jesus made clear is always revealed by the love we show.

Three Commands

Deuteronomy 7:8 tells us that God rescued the Israelites out of slavery in Egypt because of love. God saw His people in need and responded out of His love nature. Jesus took up residence on the earth to be with us because of love. Love is always the basis for interaction with us, including the reason that He saves us. "For God loved the world in this way: He gave His One and Only Son, so that everyone who believes in Him will not perish but have eternal life."[4] Love drives all of God's behaviors. And not only that, because His very essence is love, He cannot act out of any other compulsion or characteristic.

If love is what drives God's actions, and we, as His creation, reflect His image and are filled with His glory, then it has to be what drives our actions as well. If we are going to start bearing fruit that reflects His glory, we need to start understanding love in a way that is spelled G-O-D. Love has to be more than mere action or chemical reaction that provokes feelings. It has to be more than something that we associate with God, in-text, and abandon in practice. This fundamental disconnection was a huge part of how the Israelites understood and related to God.

God is Love

2

THE LAW AND LOVE

Therefore, love the Lord your God and always keep His mandate and His statutes, ordinances, and commands.
~ Deuteronomy 11:1 ~

THE LAW

613. THAT IS THE NUMBER OF COMMANDS that the Jewish people had to follow by the time Jesus showed up. From the time that Moses received the Ten Commandments until His arrival, the Jewish religious leaders had received, developed, and added 603 more laws. To be fair, many were, as we can read in the bible, received from God. But, to be even fairer, the Bible never mentions all 613 laws. It wasn't until the 3rd century that Rabbi Simlai[1] identified and listed the 613 commands that Jews were expected to and had been keeping. There's debate about the number of commands, but it's generally agreed that by the 1st century, the Pharisees were enforcing and obeying hundreds of commands, collectively referred to as "The Law."

Why so many? 613 commands do seem like a lot, especially because Moses originally received only ten. If you're not familiar with them, you can find them in Exodus 20. Even though those original 10 were given to Moses after leaving Egypt, many Jewish scholars and theologians consider significant amounts of the book of Genesis as command language. Scripture, like Genesis 1:28, "…be fruitful and multiply," is considered, by some, as a command to have children. Regardless, it would always be the Ten Commandments that would sit as the foundation of the Law. The other 603 were primarily intended to guard against disobedience of the foundational ten. Many of the added laws were mainly ceremonial and were connected to building the tabernacle and later the temple. Other commands were more akin to civil law meant to govern an Israelite theocracy and later monarchy. None of those things exist anymore, so many of the Jewish laws have been set aside for now. Whether or not some of those laws will be reestablished if a new temple is built is inconsequential, but what is important is how the law directed and influenced how the Israelite's interactions with God.

At age three, one of my daughter's favorite stories was from a Frog and Toad storybook. In this particular story, Toad bakes some cookies for him and Frog. These cookies are the best that either of them had ever eaten, and eventually, they find themselves gorging on them. Even as they say they must stop eating them, we see them stuffing more cookies into their mouths. They both agree that they need to stop eating them, so after having "one very last cookie" for the third time, Frog declares that they need will power. They quickly discover, through the continued eating of cookies, that they aren't able to muster up their own will power. Something must be done. Frog devises a plan to build barriers between them and the most delicious cookies. First, Frog places the cookies into a box, but Toad recognizes that they need only open it to eat the cookies. Frog responds by tying string around the box. Toad explains that cutting the string and opening the box would provide easy access to the cookies. Frog adds more layers, and Toad provides more "helpful" insight into how they might violate the boundaries.

Frog finally realizes that the only real way to keep from eating the cookies is to do away with them. Frog takes the box off the high shelf, cuts the string, opens the box and puts the plate of cookies outside in the yard. He then calls the birds, which swoop down and take all the cookies. With the last cookie flying away in the beak of a bird, Frog declares, "Now we have all the will power!" I love Frog and Toad stories, but this particular one made me think of this chapter because this is how the Israelites approached God's law.

Because they saw their propensity to break the law, every time it happened "one very last time," a layer was added. Eventually, they put enough buffers between them and the law, that they were unable to experience the "sweetness of His words"[2] just as Frog and Toad could not experience the most delicious cookies. These layers, or barriers, have been called fence laws. The intention was to place enough "lesser" laws in front of the central command that it mitigated the possibility of breaking the "really important" ones. The only problem was that the Israelites, like us, were really bad at following even the lesser rules and trying to be "good enough" to get God's favor. To top it all off, the law, in and of itself, wasn't even given to tell you how to "be good enough" to get to God. Paul tells us that the contrary is true. In Romans 7:7-25, he explains that the law was intended to reveal our sin to us and highlight our inability to be good enough. In fact, if you look at the way the Ten Commandments are given, they were intended to be the parameters for how to love God and love our neighbor. Commands one through five are God-honoring, while commands six through ten are other person honoring. The first five are in line with the Greatest Command, and the second five are in line with the second command, which is like it. Regardless of what the intended purpose was, like all of us, the Israelites were really bad at the whole thing.

After Frog scatters the cookies to the birds and declares, "We have lots of will power now!" Toad appears rather unimpressed. Not only is he unimpressed by all the extra will power they have recently gained, but he also has no desire to use any of it. After taking a moment, Toad turns to Frog, tells him that he can have all of the will power, and declares that he is going home to bake a cake. When it came to God's law, we can read through the Old Testament and see a similar response by the Israelites. Their process for relating to God tragically followed a particular pattern that ultimately failed them. All of the "fence" building they did, around the law, was only an attempt to "will power" themselves into obedience to the law. In the end, they would always choose to just "go make a cake."

THE OLD COVENANT CYCLE

Because of all the years that I lived inside the behavior modification form of Christianity, when I finally felt like I had hit rock bottom, I decided to abandon Christianity. My decision wasn't well thought out but was instead a very emotional response. I convinced myself that I had worked hard enough to be a good Christian and couldn't understand how that didn't translate into everything going "right" in my life. At that time, I lived inside a very conditional and transactional form of Christianity, which many still reside in today. Within days deciding to abandon Christianity, thanks to my nine-year-old son Andrew, I was back in church. It was then that I felt God whisper, "I never left." It was the first time that I felt like I belonged with God and that I could trust him. Unfortunately, I had no idea what I was supposed to do or where I was supposed to start.

When I say I didn't know what to do, I mean, even though I had read the Bible, I didn't understand how to study it, let alone develop a worldview or any kind of theology from it. Because of that, I typically did what the pastor told me that I should be doing. Because I was in the military, during that

The Law and Love

time, and law-enforcement to boot, I maintained a very analytical and linear thought process. So, I did the only thing I knew, I watched people. Specifically, I watched other Christians. As I read the Bible and learned to study it, I would watch other Christians to see if the way they were living their public life matched what I was reading in the Bible. In an attempt to figure out how I had gotten to where I was in life, I watched people and read the bible looking for clues. I know now I was working through the process that many people call deconstruction.

Mostly I was taking apart what I had learned about Christianity and God so that I could see what it was made of and if it made sense in light of scripture. I prefer to think that I was reverse engineering my faith rather than merely dismantling it. My intent was to figure out what my faith had been built from and then put it back together, but only better and more correctly this time. The difference between what I was trying to do and most other deconstruction is that with deconstruction, there's no guarantee that reconstruction will occur. And, if it does happen, you'll likely end up with something that looks completely different than Christianity. I didn't want that. I knew that I wanted to get back to the truth of who Christ is, but I wanted to understand better what it meant to live my life for Him. I also wanted to understand better what it meant to love and be loved by God. The group that provided a lot of clarity on that was the Israelites.

After some time and study, I began to see a pattern for how the Israelites interacted with God. In a word, it was kind of a mess. Within the Israelite community, they would continually violate God's law, and often in not so small ways. Because of that, they were always being punished and then groaning and wailing about their lot in life. Then, they would ask God for mercy, receive mercy, repent of their disobedience, and do it all over again. The Old Testament is replete with this vicious cycle. When I saw it, I realized that for 20 years, I had been living inside that cycle. Just that realization brought a lot of relief. Not relief that I had messed it up for 20 years, but that I knew what I was doing wrong, and because I did, I might be able to stop doing it. It also helped me feel less alone in my misunderstanding of God's desire for us. As I've worked on it over the years, here's what I've come to call the Old Covenant Cycle (Fig. 1):

GOD'S LOVE → GATHERED together → Receive the LAW → WORK to keep law → REJECT law → SEPARATION from God → GUILT → DESPAIR → REPENTANCE → MERCY → RECONCILED → GOD'S LOVE

Three Commands

I know that it seems like a lot, and it is. This way of interacting with God requires a lot of work on our part. But first, there are a few things you need to understand:

1. This entire interaction is entirely dependent on your skewed perception of what you assume God wants from you.
2. Because it's dependent on you, it heavily impedes your ability to seek a genuine relationship with God
3. Just because we messed up following the law doesn't mean God didn't intend for it to be good.

With those caveats in mind, let's get to breaking down each component. After we do, you can see the cycle in Figure 1 at the end of this section.

God's Love
As discussed, God's love is the very essence, or core, of all He is and all He does. Everything, even if we mess it up, always starts with God's love. And His love is always about having a relationship with you. We get to see this multiple times in the first chapter of Genesis: His communication with the Trinity (Let us create…), His being with Adam and Eve in the garden, and His conversation with Cain.[3]

Gathering
Throughout the Bible, we see God continually making attempts to gather His people into one unified body. Adam and Eve are the first examples of this. We see this attempt to gather continue with Abraham, Moses, through all the judges, the kings, and all the way up to Jesus gathering His disciples. God's intent and desire is to gather His people together for a mutual relationship with Him and each other.

Law
This, of course, starts with the Ten Commandments. Those 10 were eventually expanded to include 603 more. The primary purpose of these was to act as "fences" built to ensure that the original 10 were not violated. So it's clear, the law wasn't and isn't bad. It is from God, and everything from God is good. Jesus would not have said that He came to fulfill it rather than abolish it,[4] if it wasn't good. But regardless of that, in our effort to control everything, we've created a system that not only reveals but also highlights

our predisposition to break God's law. What God intended to be a good gift for forming and sustaining healthy relationships with Him and others, we used to create barriers to genuine connection within those relationships.

Work

This element speaks to our continual toil to keep the law. It speaks to the dutiful process to do all that the law requires, in an attempt to prove our qualification for heaven. The Israelites worked diligently to obey the law to prove their love for God. Unfortunately, as they did that, they lost sight of Him altogether. We can, and do, easily fall into this same mindset. When we lose focus on the Giver of the law, all we see is something that keeps us from Him. When that happens, our diligent work begins to wane and eventually becomes too much.

Rejection

The work of trying to keep the law always ends with rejecting it. We see this throughout the Old Testament in the Israelites continually walking away from God to follow other gods and cultures. And we still do it today. Although we boast that we're "not under the law," and we aren't required to keep the law, we often have lists of rules that good Christians keep. Even if this isn't your experience, many Christians operate on the assumption that they have to work if they want to be followers of Jesus. Often that plays out on Sunday mornings at church in the form of church volunteer work. It can also be seen in the many community outreach projects that churches organize. That is not to say either is bad, but that many Christians participate as a means of being involved in meaningful Christian work that will prove their love for God. Then when following the rules or doing the work becomes too overwhelming, we reject them. Surely these are two different things, rules and volunteer work, but both place a heavy burden on us. Regardless, the result is the same, people "taking a break" from church and sometimes, sadly, walking away entirely.

Separation

The Israelite's rejection of the law resulted in separation. Again, it's the same for us today. It is necessary to understand that this is not a God initiated separation. However, the bible does speak of God's glory departing from Israel and His divorce of the Northern Kingdom. Wait, what? I know, but it's right there in Jeremiah 3:8. There's a lot to that particular separation.

Three Commands

Still, Pastor David Instone-Brewer does a fantastic, and theologically honest, job of academically exploring that idea in his book, *Divorce and Remarriage in the Church*. At the heart of it, separation is initiated by the actions of the Israelites and, ultimately, us. And separation never happens quickly. It is always a slow but inevitable descent. Today, even if our departure is the result of a heavy burden placed on us by modern-day "gatekeepers" (some call them Pharisees), separation is still initiated by the person and often involves, at least for a time, distance from God.

Guilt

I don't want to say that unequivocally that everyone who experiences separation from God will experience guilt. Many have walked away and say that they didn't and don't feel guilty about it. However, their lack of guilt doesn't eliminate guilt in the process. This is particularly true if you remain inside of a faith community, specifically if you've just moved to another church, or if you've tried to maintain some of your friendships with others who haven't left. The Israelites experienced this as a collective feeling of guilt that typically involved an outside oppressive force or their exile for disobedience.

It is vital to make a distinction between healthy and unhealthy guilt. Guilt, in general, is a justified and right feeling of deserving blame because of an offense you committed; in this and the Israelite's case, the offense and ultimately every offense is committed toward God. Healthy guilt responds to the conviction of the Holy Spirit and seeks legitimate repentance and reconciliation. Guilt becomes unhealthy when we allow the enemy to use it to invoke shame, which draws you farther from God. Regardless, in the end, guilt left unchecked is a heavy burden that brings with it further depths of separation and potentially a long spiral into despair.

Despair

For the Israelites, despair was a typical result of their shame-ridden guilt caused by separation from God. This desperation was often seen in the people's pleading with the prophets to seek God on their behalf. They needed to be back with God, if only for relief from their circumstances. Regardless, we could easily see that they were desperate to return to Him. Today, we can more readily see the desperation for meaning, which, whether we can admit it or not, is desperation for God. We still handle it in the same way as the Israelites, except instead of prophets, we defer to church pastors.

The Law and Love

Repentance
In the Old Testament, this was most often a communal process that was very closely tied to the law. Once the Israelites became desperate enough, typically, the leader (usually the king) would go to the prophet and ask them to seek God's forgiveness. At that point, God would set the parameters for repentance, and they would perform those acts. For the Israelites, this process was more about legal requirements and less about the heart. The idea was that if they returned and adhered to the demands of the law, they would return to a better quality of life. Repentance wasn't about a desire to be with God in a relationship, it was about the desire to no longer be punished. We can still easily fall into this view of repentance; only we do it from a bargaining mindset. Usually, it takes the form of "I'll quit doing _____ if You just help me this time." Of course, it's likely a really good thing to stop the behavior that's causing the separation from God, but when we offer to cease it as a form of concession to get back in God's "good graces," we miss the point of repentance entirely.

Mercy
This was always God's primary response to His people. Even when the Israelites sought to appease Him through law directed sacrifices, with their primary purpose being to better their current situation, God still responded with mercy. The Israelite's obedience always drew God's mercy, which is driven by His grace for us. Mercy continues to be His response today. Even when we get things "wrong" or we "fail," His mercy and grace are readily available to us. Unfortunately, we don't often recognize either because we are more likely to be driven by the process of pleasing God rather than motivated by a desire for a relationship with Him.

Reconciled
Reconciliation is always God's desired end. In the case of the Israelites, they could hasten or delay the reunion with God, based on their willingness to adhere to the requirements for reconciliation. We're given the same type of choice as well. Unfortunately, for the Northern Kingdom (Israel), they would not choose reconciliation. God repeatedly called them back to His side, but they rejected the requirements of it, which resulted in God issuing them a certificate of divorce and sending them away, never to return.[5] Alternatively, those who did work through the process were restored into a relationship

with God. Historically this process was acted out on a national scale, being largely a communal and ceremonial event. Today, however, because of Jesus' work on the cross, it has been personalized into largely an individual process.

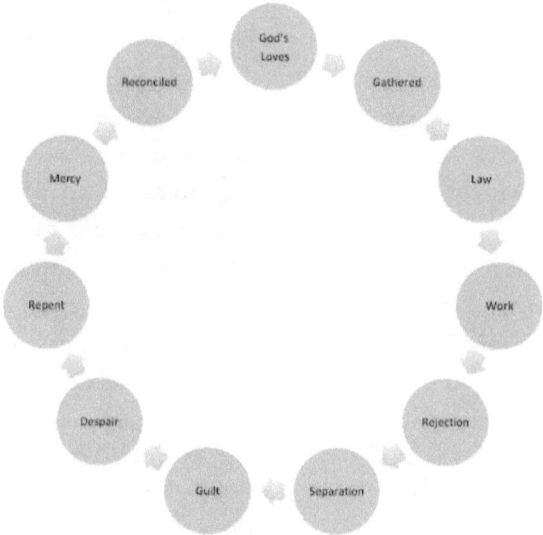

Figure 1, Old Covenant Cycle

Because the Israelites often got it wrong, they would stay stuck in this Old Covenant cycle. But despite that, God still used it to reveal His love and gather His people under that love. Once gathered, He showed them how He planned to set them apart, as unique and separate, from the rest of the world, for the Israelites, which was the purpose of the law. Regardless of the intent of the law, the Israelites wouldn't allow it to be the light that guided them toward loving God and their neighbors well. Instead, it became a measuring stick for who was holier and was often used to keep people from God. In approaching it that way, the law became more of a focus than God, and their loyalty and reverence was to it first. That view of the law required them to add layers of other requirements to it, lest the common man figured out how to approach God. Eventually, that practice becomes too burdensome, and the response to most burdens is outright rejection, a casting off if you will. When rejection happens, rebellion isn't typically too far behind.

Here is an example of this cycle in action. When we realize that the actual object of our rebellion is God, Himself, in many cases, we feel guilt. Unfortunately, guilt is one of the things that the Enemy knows well, and he often uses it to evoke shame as a way to create further separation from God.

The Law and Love

As the chasm of separation widens, a crisis point eventually comes. It is a crisis that often invites despair, and it is despair that causes us to remember and desire our past blessings. Despair can be a great motivator, so it follows that out of desperation, we call out to God for relief. We bargain, plead, and beg for His mercy. We go to the people we think have exclusive access to God; in the past, it was prophets or priests, today it's pastors, and beseech them for the right gifts to offer, hoping that God will relent and pour out His mercy.

And what do they have to offer us, but His word? It's His word that calls us to repentance and is always beckoning us to turn back and go the way He has directed. So we repent. We change our minds and turn away from the chasm of separation. And because of God's abounding and infinite grace, He pours out His mercy and greets our return with a robe, ring, sandals, and a feast. We experience reconciliation until the work becomes too much again.

That's the cycle the Israelites, and we, get stuck in when we try to approach God by viewing Him through the Old Covenant. Phil Vischer, the creator of *Veggie Tales* and *What's in the Bible* and co-host of *The Holy Post* podcast, calls this, "Old Testament living." And God knows that we see the law this way and that we get stuck in this cycle. He watched the Israelites get stuck in it for thousands of years. It's for that reason that Jesus came. He came to give us a new lens through which to see everything in the Kingdom: the law, others, ourselves, and even God. And without that lens, we always have and will continue to view God incorrectly and hence, approach Him incorrectly.

OUR INCORRECT VIEWS OF GOD

The song, "Good, Good Father," written by Pat Barrett and recorded by Chris Tomlin debuted at the end of 2015 and was an instant hit on the Sunday morning worship circuit. It was so widely popular that the joke was that any church music set list had to include it as the opening and closing song if they wanted to be taken seriously. Despite all the joking, it really is a great song. I still get choked up when I listen to it, and I know a lot of people who it affects that same way. I'm convinced that it affects people this way because deep down, we all understand the importance of having a good father. And even though we know this and declared how good of a Father God is, for 47 Sundays in a row, we often still struggle with actually believing it. In fact, many of us live as if we believe other opposing views of God.

Three Commands

Before I continue, I want to acknowledge that there are a lot of healthy ways that many people view God. Those who have a healthy view of God may feel that this section doesn't apply to them and that they can skip ahead; I would implore you not to. If you have any inclination to participate in or be a part of a Christian community, you will undoubtedly interact with people who have one or all of these views of God, and it will only benefit your relationships to understand these views.

I also want to acknowledge that there are a lot of other unhealthy ways that people can, and do, view God. I selected these three because these are the ones that I've heard most often and ones that I think share a specific element that keeps people trapped in these unhealthy views. That element is fear. And since this is a book about love, and perfect love casts out fear,[6] it seemed appropriate to address three specific views. Those three are God as a Harsh Taskmaster, as an Angry Father, and as a Merciless Judge.

It isn't always clear if fear produces these views of God or if fear is the fruit of these views and serves to perpetuate them. Surely these views of God can be adopted for any number of reasons, but what is clear is that fear does play a central role in a person relating to God from one of these three views. Concerning these views, I'm not talking about being afraid of God, although that does happen, but rather the "fear of not." The "fear of not" is the fear that you may not have a specific need fulfilled, so it drives you toward striving to have that need met. Within the context of these views, we can see the fear of not doing enough, not being loved, and not being seen as good. In not having these three needs (to be enough, to be loved, and to be good), a person can get trapped in viewing and relating to God in these ways.

Harsh Taskmaster

If you're not familiar with the Israelite's history with God, first, go read your Bible. But, for now, you need to know that they spent 400 years as slaves in Egypt, before receiving the law. Eventually, God freed them from Pharaoh's grip and began leading them through the wilderness to the land that He promised Abraham long before they were ever slaves. To understand this view of God, as a harsh taskmaster, we need to understand the gravity of Israel's time spent in Egypt.

As I already mentioned, I grew up in a large Italian family. If you know anything about Italians, then you know two crucial things. First, it's not a sauce, it's gravy. Second, we're loud. And when I say aloud, I mean shouting all the time type loud. It doesn't matter what we're doing; talking, "whispering" during a movie, throwing a party, arguing about almost

The Law and Love

anything, we're just loud. And I grew up learning, from every family member, that we're "loud people." I've even instilled that in my sons. The fact that we're loud has been passed down, consistently, for generations. That's what I've always known to be true about us as a people group. It wasn't until my early 30s that I figured out that we didn't need to be loud. But it was so ingrained in me that when I am loud, and someone comments on it, my conditioned response is, "I'm Italian." The beautiful part about that is that most people accept that as a reasonable answer.

You can take any mentality and repeat it over and over and over for generations and generations, and it will become an ingrained mindset. In the case of the Israelites, replace being loud with being a slave as a mindset. It's what they knew as a people group. Millions of people, for generations, only knew the slavery they were born into. When God rescued them out of Egypt, the slave mindset was so ingrained in them, as a people, that they interacted with God out of that mindset. Numerous times throughout their trek through the wilderness, we read about the Israelites complaining about the difficulty of the wilderness. Embedded in their complaint was always the mindset that it would've been better to live as slaves in Egypt, then to "die" in the wilderness with God. They even considered going back to Egypt on multiple occasions.

It wasn't just the verbalization of their desire to return to Egypt that revealed their slavery mindset. Early in their exodus from Egypt, God desired to speak directly to the people of Israel. And In Deuteronomy 5:24–27, we see their slave mindset revealed. It's in this small passage of scripture that the people tell Moses that they fear hearing God's voice because they are afraid they will die. In response, they ask Moses to speak with God and "then speak to us all that the Lord our God speaks to you, and we will hear and do it."

The Israelites are given the opportunity to have a personal relationship with God but instead opt for an intermediary. They viewed God the same way they understood Pharaoh while they were in Egypt. They would never speak directly with Pharaoh, but would instead take orders from the soldiers who drove their daily work. In fact, Pharaoh, the ultimate taskmaster, would give orders to the head taskmaster, who gave orders to the soldiers, and who would give orders to the slaves. Their job as slaves was to hear and do. This verse reveals that they viewed God in the same way; tell us and we'll do it. This was the mindset of a slave. The Israelites viewed God from a place of doing to please and appease. The fear of not doing enough painted the way they saw and related to God and whether or not they thought He was pleased with them. For the Israelites, God's pleasure was primarily based on if they did enough for Him.

We can see that mindset persists even when Jesus shows up. In Luke 10, Jesus goes to visit Mary and Martha. It's important to understand that the sisters both believed Jesus was the Messiah they had been waiting for. When Jesus arrives at their home, Mary chooses to sit at Jesus' feet and listen to Him speak, while Martha busies herself with cleaning and preparing a meal. Instead of focusing on being with Jesus, Martha's assumption was that He would prefer her to be busy with performing tasks that would earn His approval. But Jesus calls this out. He tells Martha that Mary has found the thing that matters, by sitting at His feet. In this, He is addressing her mindset that she needs to do means of receiving His approval.

We still do this today. We've become a church full of Marthas, busying ourselves with everything we assume God needs or wants us to do. We make statements like, "used by God" and call our work "sacrifice" for the Lord, counting each completed task as a Christ-like scar, caused by the great taskmaster's whip. It becomes our badge and the evidence of our commitment to God. In doing so, it's clear that we continually seek the "attaboy/girl" instead of hearing that He's already saying, "That's my boy/girl."

Angry Father

Of all the unhealthy ways to view God, likely the most damaging is seeing Him as an angry father. Most often, we take this view because we paint the face of our earthly father on God. Whether he was present in our life or not, our earthly father is often the primary reference we have for what a father should be. Author and speaker, Rick Thomas, talks about how a young child is only able to apply one label to any one object. Because of this, a child cannot consider that it is possible to apply multiple labels to the same object. When we extend that to how we view a father, Thomas suggests, "a child develops his label, definition, and interpretation of a father by observing his own father." This is where a child develops his or her label for "father." Because of that, Thomas points out, "[a child] understands what God the Father is like through the attitudes, words, and actions of his earthly father."

It is this view in which a person has experienced the adverse effects of a really unhealthy father or father figure. On some level, the child's father figure primarily expressed the singular emotion, anger. That frequent anger likely caused the child to feel unloved, which was a contradiction to how they knew or at least assumed, parents were supposed to love and interact with

The Law and Love

their children. As a result of the child's fear of not being loved, they likely responded in ways that they hoped would garner their father's love. Sadly, because of the seemingly ever-present anger, the child will often go without and in the process learns to tiptoe on eggshells so as not to suffer the father's fury.

When a person's image of a father is built by on the poor or hurtful image of their earthly father, they typically transfer that to God the Father. The lasting effects of this developed label can be seen in many adult Christians who strive to not make God angry so as not to incur His wrath. Unfortunately, they do not typically keep this view of God to themselves. Usually, often done unintentionally, they have no problem communicating to others just how angry God is. This is a problem in and of itself but becomes the most damaging with their children and new Christians. They are essentially locking other people in the room with them as they quietly cower in the corner, lest they make father angry. They don't mean to do it, but it's what they know, and a person can only communicate what they know. Viewing God as an angry father keeps them trapped in the Old Covenant process. They follow the rules out of fear of making God angry. When they fail, they feel guilty, then run and/or hide from Him. Because they desperately desire to be with their Father, they do what we think is required to appease Him. Their act of loyalty is to go back to following the familiar rules. Sadly they're more intimately familiar with the rules than they are with their Father.

Merciless Judge

A third way we view God, which I'll address, is as a merciless judge. This view is primarily based on the person's fear that they are not good; and not "good enough," but really just not good. I need to be clear on two things here. First, I'm not suggesting that people are intrinsically good. The bible straight up says that no one is righteous. That scripture more points to the fact that no one is in right standing with God, but it still makes the point that we're not good. I'm talking about the fear of not being good, as in redeemable and worthy of Jesus' work on the cross. While we may not have been in right standing before God, the bible also makes clear that we are a good and, in fact, a very good creation. This view of God comes when we don't believe that we are God's good creation, made in His image, and worthy of Christ's work.

Second, the Bible also straight-up calls God a Judge, specifically a just judge. The Bible is explicit that all people will eventually give an account to

God as a Judge. So, there's no doubt that He is a judge and will judge all things. Ultimately this is a good thing. Without Him as Judge, His word is meaningless. And thankfully, His word is never meaningless. If this was the only view of Him as a judge, we'd be okay. Unfortunately, it's not.

When we let fear mold our view of God as a merciless judge, we become obsessed with following the rules. And not that following rules is a bad thing; on the contrary, rules are essential and for our benefit. But when fear of not being good is our motivation, rule-following becomes the focus and forces out genuine grace and forgiveness when we inevitably fail. Our fear causes us to strictly, as much as possible, adhere to doing for Him rather than being with Him. This view results in us quickly rejecting God's abundant grace because grace rarely sneaks into the rules and structure of judgment. In this case, the fear that keeps us following the rules almost always results in anger toward others who don't. It's not enough that we've bound ourselves to a God of judgment who, if we falter, is bent on our destruction; we need others to be bound to the same judge. If they are, then everything is fair. They don't get away with anything that we don't. And heaven forbid if they commit an offense against us; God will surely smite them because He is a just God, punishing those who hate the righteous. Regardless of which of these views we apply to God, the focus is always on behavior. Fortunately for us, God is a just judge and far more concerned about our positioning with Him, than our ability to do what appeases His judgment.

IF YOU LOVE ME, THEN... BE GOOD

The Gospel of Behavior Modification
When I first became a Christian, the church at large was in a weird place. Like many Christians, most of what I knew came from what I heard the pastor preach on Sunday. I never opened my bible, except for reading as part of my parent's misconduct rehabilitation program, which often included reading the book of Numbers. There was no mid-week small group to "go deeper," and Wednesday youth was mainly skateboarding and soda, with a salvation message tacked on to the end of the evening. And, because my parents became Christians at the same time as I did, there wasn't a concept of discipleship, which meant we didn't do things like family devotionals, pray together, read or even talk about the bible.

Instead, I sat in church on Sundays, sometimes on Wednesdays, and listened to a pastor tell me what it took to be a good Christian. The technical

The Law and Love

term for putting all your energy into reforming your behavior is behavior modification. It seemed as if most of the sermons I was hearing were focused on the things that I shouldn't be doing. The pastor never outright said it, but it was always implied that we needed to change our behavior to please God. How we ended up there, as a church, really doesn't matter; what matters is that we did. It matters because of what it communicated to the Church about God, His character, and His desire for us.

For most of my early years as a Christian, I was led to believe, whether directly or indirectly, that my behavior impacted God accepting me. It isn't that grace wasn't preached, it was, but it always seemed as if it was measured out based on me acting "right." Sadly, my relationship with Jesus suffered for a long time because of this. This is how Jesus ended up in the periphery of my Christianity. Please do not misunderstand me. I am not placing all of the blame for my shortcomings in following Jesus on the church. I include myself in having responsibility for that failure. Regardless of the church's handling, or mishandling of discipleship, individually, I am not excused from my responsibility for seeking knowledge of Jesus and choosing to follow Him. With responsibility rightly placed, much of my rejection of Jesus' call to follow Him had to do with the difficulty of adhering to the seemingly never-ending "don't do" list. It was almost as if we'd established our own version of the 613 laws.

There were rules like "no 'R' rated movies." Absolutely no movies with cursing, violence and/or gore were allowed. Obviously, any film with nudity was a huge no-no. "No school dances" because they were billed as the "devil's playground," although I went anyway. There were music rules, too. Like "no pop or rock music," which is an impossible task when you grew up in the 80s & 90s – I mean seriously, Don't Stop Believing, My Own Personal Jesus and Thriller, need I say more? Regardless, the list of rules felt overwhelming. They weren't written down anywhere, but we all knew them; we heard them every week. Christian life became so restrictive that it was impossible to feel like I was ever a good Christian, which is what drove my need to "get saved" every other Wednesday and at every youth camp. Because of that, I saw so many kids my age, and many adults, just "playing" church. Eventually, many would end up walking away from it.

Every time I went to church, it seemed like there was another thing added to that list. I didn't realize it at the time, but every time something was added, it caused me to buck harder against that system of control. As far as I was concerned, I was just rebelling against a system. Unfortunately, and I didn't realize it then, but for me, it wasn't just that. I was actually rejecting Christ's

Three Commands

bride, and by proxy, Christ Himself. At the time, it seemed justified because Christianity appeared to be moving backward toward following the law. It was becoming primarily about behavior modification. The theology we were given was, "just stop doing the stuff that Christians don't do, then you'll be good and acceptable to God." So, since cursing offended Jesus, don't do it. Drunkenness was obviously offensive to Jesus, so get saved and just stop. If you smoked cigarettes, that clearly made God angry, so stop it. The list was, and still is in many cases, a long one. The implication was if you weren't delivered from your bad behavior and couldn't stop doing whatever it was that kept you from being a good Christian, it was due to one of two reasons: you weren't trying hard enough, or you weren't really saved. And if followed to the logical conclusion, both reasons were just code for either not having enough faith in Jesus or worse, not loving Him at all.

I am in no way suggesting that, as Christians, we can do whatever we want or that behavior doesn't matter or have consequences. I believe in watching what we put into our minds and hearts for the sake of our soul and spirit. There are absolutely things that are useful and beneficial and other things that damage the very core of who we are, and it's certainly biblical to believe that. In 1 Corinthians 10:23, Paul said, "You say, 'I am allowed to do anything, but not everything is good for you. You say, 'I am allowed to do anything, but not everything is beneficial." It comes down to the truth that we cannot merely abuse God's grace by doing whatever we want and think that everything will turn out fine.

Unfortunately, if the focus of a relationship is what you're not allowed to do, you miss the wonder of what you're participating in. Needless to say, all the rules made it easy to come up with reasons for why I didn't want to be "that kind of Christian." That mindset helped me slide down the slippery slope of abusing God's grace. I would tell myself, "God loves me, and He'll always forgive me," and then I'd use my newly cleared conscience to go out and do more stupid stuff. As accurate as it is that God will always forgive us, I routinely used it as a license to sin, knowing I could just "repent" and ask for forgiveness, making everything all right. As I got older, it was easier to live inside that lie, to the point that I didn't even make excuses for my behavior anymore. I simply lived under shallow grace and the motto, "only God can judge me." By 31 years old, with my life and marriage starting to collapse, I was exhausted. Mostly I was exhausted from trying to figure out which rules I had to follow and how grace actually worked. At that point in my life, I was utterly trapped in the Old Covenant cycle and ready to let my separation from God end in divorce.

THE APOSTLES ON BEING "GOOD"

God intended for the Old Covenant to be a good thing, a promise of a mutually loving relationship built on our reconciliation to God. The problem is that we somehow couldn't stomach the simplicity of it and turned it into something so burdensome that rejection was the more comfortable choice. Maybe it isn't that we couldn't stomach it, but that we were fearful of it. And not in the good "fear of the Lord leads to wisdom" kind of way. But in the dangerous way that leads people to do horrible and sometimes repugnant things. While fear-filled people have propagated all of the horrors of the world, their fear pales in comparison to the kind that causes us to continually separate ourselves from the source of life and love.

Because of fear--fear of breaking the rules, fear of angering God, fear of loss, fear of consequences--we built systems that ensure our "goodness." The collective 613 laws were one of those systems. Other similar systems might include the Catholic practices of penance, or paying indulgences as a means of lessening punishment for sin. These systems are intended to ensure that we don't break the core rules, lest we be condemned to eternal punishment. If we do, we come up with ways to mitigate or reduce the penalty. In essence, these systems are our attempts at being our own savior. In doing so, we make being good or good enough our ultimate aim. The problem with that is we were never meant to be good. Not only that, the bible is clear that, through the law, we aren't capable of being good. Romans 3:10-12 says, "None is righteous, no, not one; no one understands; no one seeks for God. All have turned aside; together they have become worthless; no one does good, not even one." Neither Jesus nor the Apostles tell us that we're supposed to be good. Instead, they continually talk about being made new. Paul makes this clear in the latter parts of Romans 3 by reiterating that it is through Christ and His work that we are justified and made new. Paul is continually saying that we are new creations.[7] And Peter tells us that we are now partakers in God's divine nature.[8] He tells us that it's only by grace that we enter into this newness.

The good news and truth is, everything we do fits under grace. Even when we don't want it, grace is still there, waiting for us to take hold of it. In my younger self's early attempts to throw off the oppressive weight of a rule laden church, I was tossing away a relationship where love and grace abound. I was tired of trying to be good enough and had figured out what Israel likely figured out millennia before me; specifically, following the law is hard, and you are never good enough. In the end, Jesus didn't say, "If you love me, be good." He said, "…obey my commands." That can be confusing, especially after discussing just how difficult following the law is. But it isn't about being good enough. It's about being made into a new creation with a nature that moves toward obedience. Jesus had something different in mind when He spoke about being born again. In truth, it really wasn't different or new in the sense that it hadn't previously existed in God's desire for us. Instead, it would be a command that would not only fulfill the requirements of the Law but bring a unity that God's people had never previously experienced. But, for us to truly grasp and carry out Jesus' New Command, we have to understand where our ability to love comes from. We are only capable of loving in that way because He first loved us.

The Law and Love

3

HE FIRST LOVED US

We love because He first loved us.
~ 1 John 4:19 ~

FOR A LONG TIME NOT ONLY did I not understand what it meant that God loved us first, I didn't necessarily believe it. I was 14 years old the first time I heard it and I remember thinking, "There's no way God loves me just because."

At the church where I first became a Christian, they practiced the Gifts of the Holy Spirit. Depending on who you ask, those gifts are: the word of wisdom, the word of knowledge, increased faith, the gifts of healing, the gift of miracles, prophecy, the discernment of spirits, diverse kinds of tongues, and interpretation of tongues. These gifts are popular with, and often the distinguishing factor of, the charismatic/Pentecostal side of Evangelicalism. Some denominations and Christians believe they were only necessary for the Apostles in establishing the early church and have since ceased. I'm not going to get into the theology behind that, but I'll say this, I've seen a number of those gifts used and it seemed pretty real. But, it wasn't always that way.

At 14 years old I had been a Christian for about two years. Over those years I attended our Wednesday night youth group and was struggling, like a lot of people I've known, with understanding what it meant to be "saved." Personally, I think I responded to the call for salvation every week. One of the benefits of preaching behavior modification is that keeps the altars full. Again, one of the gifts is speaking in diverse kinds of tongues. This is typically understood in two ways. One is that the speaker, through the power of Holy Spirit, is able to speak an actual foreign language that they didn't previously know. That would be the equivalent to me being able to speak German without having taken a German language class. The other understanding is that speaking in tongues is to speak in a divine language that the speaker, and others around the speaker, doesn't understand. Characteristically, this form of tongues doesn't sound like actual words. In the first case the intent is to equip you to preach the Gospel to someone in his or her native language. In the second, the intent is most often to use it as a private prayer language, although some churches speak it out over the congregation in conjunction with someone interpreting it.

During those first two years, I had seen a number of people use this gift publicly. Not only that, the church leaders talked about it as if it was the defining gift for being "baptized" in or filled with the Holy Spirit. The implication was, and often still is, that you may have received the Holy Spirit, but speaking in tongues was the evidence of your baptism in Him and of His power in you. On one particular Wednesday night, the youth pastor asked students if they wanted to be "filled with the Spirit." When you're young and trying to figure out what it means to be a "good" Christian, you answer "Yes" to a question like that. So I did. As the pastor spoke and prayed for us to be "filled," a number of students began to speak in tongues. I don't remember if the feeling was invoked by my youth pastor or my friends, maybe both, but I felt an expectation from others for me to speak. So I faked it. I began mumbling sounds and they bought it.

When I got home that night I remember crying. It wasn't uncontrolled sobbing, but more like those tears that stream down your face from a deep place of hurt, and I thought, "I just faked the Holy Spirit. There's no way God loves me." Worse than that, I felt like I had no one I could tell, lest I be chastised. Because I felt I couldn't tell anyone, I also had no one to correct my understanding. I carried that belief for the next 18 years. For most of that time I actually thought that God was angry with me, and was withholding Holy Spirit from me. For almost two decades I couldn't fathom a world where I could mess up and still have God see me in a loving way, let alone as a righteous person. One of my favorite things about the Apostle Paul is that he had this amazing understanding of his own duplicity. We know that he was both, at the same time, the worst of sinners[1] and the righteousness of God.[2] He was confident in that understanding, and that idea moved him deeper into Jesus, deeper into His grace and deeper into His love. Paul understood that God's love meant He wasn't angry with him and that He accepted him into the body. Not because, or even despite his past, but because of who he was in Christ. Through that example and the challenging of wrong beliefs, I'm reaching the same type of understanding.

All that to say, it took that single event for me to believe that God was angry with me beyond His capacity to love me. And it didn't affect just me. Accepting that lie impacted the way I loved or didn't love, others. And worse, it impacted my ability to receive and then reflect love. I know a lot of people that share the same belief about His love for them. The saddest part about that truth is that our ability to love others, including God, comes from our realization and acceptance of His love for us. Without knowing the depth of His love for us, we cannot love in any real or meaningful way.

GOD LOVES THE WORLD

It would be wrong not to have this as our starting point for God's love. In John 3:16, Jesus said, "For God loved the world in this way: He gave His One and Only Son, so that everyone who believes in Him will not perish but have eternal life." Jesus, God the Son, is telling us why He came to earth, and He opens with "God loved the world." It was God's love that drove His action toward our reconciliation with Him. The Gospel message starts with love. And, because the natural inclination of love is to give, we see this in His very next words; "He gave." Again, notice that this is an accurate estimation, adequate supply, and carries no expectation.

If God is love and love is inclined to give, then an obvious and natural action of God would be to give. My love for my wife and children prompts me to want to provide them with everything. Of course, the desire to raise decent and unselfish human beings encourages my better judgment not to give my kids whatever they want. But, that doesn't change the fact that I love giving gifts to my children. If it's within my power to do it, I want to do it for them.

Right before my oldest son turned 20, he called and asked me to drive him to Arizona. He had been living and working in the Seattle area for a couple of years and was doing okay. But, he figured it was time to go to college and, having some friends who lived there, decided that Arizona was a good place to begin adulting. Of course, I said I would, without completely understanding the scale of his request. So, I woke up early on a Saturday morning, drove the 8 hours from my home in Boise, picked him up, then spent all day Sunday driving back home. The next weekend, we decided to leave Friday after I got off work so I could make it back before Monday morning. So, I went to work on Friday with a packed car, worked all day, and then we started our 14-hour drive to Arizona.

It's worth mentioning that because he had just gotten his license the day before we left, he wasn't comfortable driving, so I drove the whole way. That weekend I drove 14 hours, with a 4-hour stop to sleep, and arrived at his new place around 4 pm. After eating at In-N-Out, being from SoCal requires me to visit whenever I'm in proximity to one, I started my trek back, only stopping to sleep in my car for 3 hours along the way.

In 36 hours, I had driven for over 28 hours, tossed and turned while trying to sleep in a car for about a total of 7 hours, and arrived home utterly exhausted. In reality, my son probably could have figured out how to get there by himself. It might have cost the same or been cheaper and took less time for him to figure out another way. But, he was nervous about moving and asked me to be with him. Because I love him, I gave my son what he asked for and probably needed.

I share that story to make this point: for all the good gifts we give to our children pale in comparison to the gift that God has given us in Christ. In Matthew 7, Jesus said, "If you then, who are evil, know how to give good gifts to your children, how much more will your Father in heaven give good things to those who ask Him!" Notice that Jesus isn't asking a question. He's making a statement about God directing His goodness toward us to eclipse our understanding of what it looks like to give in the name of love. He makes it sound as if giving is a basic tenant and the natural and primary way that God relates to us when it comes to love.

WHAT YOU NEED, NOT WHAT YOU DESERVE

Jesus' words in Matthew 7 could be interpreted as asking God for almost anything. But Jesus is talking about Himself as the ultimate good gift. He then begins talking about the Kingdom of God, so it seems logical that He is likely referring back to God answering Israel's request for a king in the Old Testament. In 1 Samuel 8:5, the people of Israel asked for a king saying, "…appoint a king to judge us the same as all the other nations have." God wasn't too happy about this. He was their King, and they were asking for a human one to replace Him. Even though God saw this as a direct and intentional rejection of Him, He still granted their request. He told Samuel to give the people what they wanted but instructed him to warn them about all the "rights" a human king would exert as he ruled over them. From that point, things weren't very good for Israel. There was continuous war, many of their kings were poor (some outright horrible) rulers, they adopted the cultural and religious practices of the nations around them. They were eventually exiled from their land on more than one occasion, with the north Kingdom ultimately being utterly destroyed.

Although most of the Israelite's experience with a human king wasn't good, it wasn't all bad. There were kings, weaved throughout their early history, who tried to lead the nation toward God. Often they would gain some success in doing so, only to have the people rebel again. Regardless of His people's continued failure, God still desired to fulfill His promise to give them, and us, the gift of a good King. Enter Jesus. Jesus is the King that all of humankind desires, even if we don't or won't acknowledge Him as such. He is the King that will lead us into the Father's Kingdom. He is the King who came to serve, not be served. He is the good gift that reunites us with the Father. It is in the "giving of His Son" that we see the clearest picture of God's love for the world.

In his book *Four Loves*, C.S. Lewis introduces this idea by identifying two types of love: Gift-love and Need-love. Gift-love is divine love. It is the type of love that drives every action of God. Lewis says that Gift-love can be "vaguely seen" in the man who works hard to plan and save for his family's future, knowing he will die without ever sharing or seeing the benefit. It is a love that is selfless and always directed toward the gain of others. If Gift-love is a love that gives, then Need-love is the love to which it responds. Need-love, Lewis explains, is the love that drives a frightened child into the arms of his mother. He goes on to explain that Need-love is not "bad" in a general sense, but is instead the type of love that drives us to God. It is the love, that when properly understood, causes our selfishness to be attracted to the selflessness of God's good gift.

Did I just say that Need-love is selfish? Yes, but not in a negative way, we tend to see the word. By its very nature, it's a love that requires something from someone else. Need-love can be a destructive kind of love, but need in itself isn't an exclusively bad thing. There are undoubtedly more than two kinds of love, but Lewis starts the book with delineating between gift-love and need-love because they are the basis for all of our interactions with God and ultimately with the rest of His creation. Because God operates from a love that gives good gifts as a response to our need, Jesus comes as the perfect personification of Give-love. He is the gift that we need, even when we think we deserve something else. Unfortunately, the conflict between what we need and what we believe we deserve springs from a more profound questioning about whether we are lovable.

He First Loved Us

ARE WE LOVABLE?

Most of us just want the answer to be a simple "yes." If we're lovable, not only should people love us, but it means we also deserve love. Even though many people believe they don't deserve love, no one wants to be unloved. And, though some people might never use 'lovable' to describe themselves, we see the desire to be loved in our confusion, hurt, or offense when someone doesn't like us. I can't count the times that I've thought, "What did I do to them? I was only ever nice." Or "They don't like me?! They don't even know me. Screw them. I'm a great guy." We like to think we're lovable, but the truth is, there's probably plenty of stuff about us that isn't lovable. But does that mean we're not lovable ourselves? Yes, and no.

One of my all-time favorite books is *Divine Romance* by Gene Edwards. The prose is so poetic and almost reads like the script of a play. The book tells the story of God's desire for His bride, which is measured out through His creation of the world and proceeds through Jesus' resurrection. The whole book revolves around the singular idea that God desires to love His bride and for His bride to love Him back. In helping to explain why God created us, ultimately to be gathered as one body, as His bride, Edwards writes this about God creating Eve for Adam,

> Man shall now have one beside him. One of his very substance, his being extended. I shall now build flesh from his flesh. Bone from his bone. Thus shall he gain a counter-part. A counter-part who is oneness. A counter-part on whom he may pour out his love."

Edwards is using reflective language here. He is communicating that God desires a counter-part on whom He can pour out His love.

At the time that God built Eve out of Adam's side, it was an image of what He would do with His Church, through the work of the second Adam, Jesus. He was showing us that He is intent on building us, His people, into one body so that we would be His bride; His very own Eve. That was the message that Paul was communicating to the Corinthian church, and us, when he said, "...I have promised you in marriage to one husband – to present a pure virgin to Christ."[3] He is clearly saying that we, the church, are going to be presented to Christ in the same way that a bride is given to her husband. We are being built together as the bride of Christ, created for the explicit purpose of God pouring out His love on us. And that is what makes us lovable. God created us to be joined together, with each other and Jesus, so that we would be loved. It's that simple. We are lovable because He loves us. Unfortunately, many do not live inside of that truth.

In that same declaration to the Corinthian church, Paul laments his fear for them by saying, "But I fear that, as the serpent deceived Eve by his cunning, your minds may be seduced from a complete and pure devotion to Christ."[4] In this passage, Paul shares his concern about the Bride falling for the cunning of people who were teaching a false Jesus. He's afraid that the people of Corinth, and eventually we, might be deceived into joining ourselves with something or someone other than the true Bridegroom. Once deceived, we begin to believe that we do not deserve the love of a good God, and that is when we become convinced that we are unlovable.

Even though God has made it clear time and again, that He created us for love, we somehow buy the lie. We look in the mirror and believe we are less than what God desires and calls us to be. We accept lesser versions of the truth and reject the one that makes us lovable. It was never that we were unlovable, but rather that we are separated from the One who makes us lovable. C.S. Lewis answers the question of how lovable we are by saying, "God loves us; not because we are lovable but because He is love, not because He needs to receive, but because He delights to give."[5] In realizing that we are lovable, we become reflections of that love.

REFLECTING LOVE

In *Divine Romance*, after saving the Israelites out of Egypt, God has them camp at the base of Mt. Sinai, where Moses will receive the Law from Him. As God walks through their camp, among His people, He hears them declare all that they will do for Him because He saved them. There are promises of gold, worship, service, and sacrifice. After hearing the grandiosity of their offering, a saddened God sits and groans in sorrow. In His sorrow He proclaims,

> I did not require of you your wealth nor coins of gold.
> What need have I of these?
> I did not ask of you that you serve me.
> Do I, the Mighty One, need to be waited upon?
> Neither did I ask of you your worship nor your prayers nor even your obedience.
> I have asked this of you,
> **that you love me...**

love me...
love me.[6]

When God created us in His image, one of the primary characteristics He placed in us was His love essence. In doing so, he intended that we would always reflect this love to Him. God simply desired that our response to His love be for us to love Him back. He does not want our silver and gold. He wants us to return the love freely that He gives freely. Because He created us in His image, God desires, and will always desire, for us to respond to Him and others with love. And not just love, but a love grounded in and built out of a relationship with Him. Reflecting God's love, back to Him, and projecting it, toward others, is why Jesus says, "What you do for the least of these you did for Me."[7]

If we're created to reflect His love, does that mean we're "wired" to love? Is it a part of our nature, and if so, shouldn't it come naturally? If you believe Genesis 1:27, then yes, it is, or at least it was intended to be. If God's essence is love, and we are reflective of His image, then it is also part of our essence. But, if that's true, then why are we so bad at loving God and others well? That's where "fallen nature" comes in. The fall caused our separation from Love, Himself. Once separated from the source of love, we're less likely to reflect or project that kind of love.

God intends for His people to love above and beyond what would be considered reasonable by human standards. I used to ask myself, "If God is love, why don't people love better?" That was before I cared about a relationship with God. I may not have known Jesus well, but I knew what the bible said, and I had a hard time understanding why I couldn't just muster up the ability to love well. In reality, I didn't feel loved and needed to know why. What made it worse was that I knew, and still know, people who love others well. And I mean ridiculously well. And some of those people weren't even Christian. How is that possible? I think it's a valid question and draws us to an important point. Even though someone can love well without believing in God, it doesn't mean that the ability to love doesn't originate with Him. It does. It always does.

OUR HUMAN CAPACITY TO LOVE

Mr. Eaton was my 5th-grade teacher. He was always kind. He reminded me of Mr. Rogers. I was 10 and 11 years old at the time, and I remember that I loved being around him. I think back and realize that I wanted to be around

Three Commands

him because compassion and patience poured out of him. Even after I left the 5th grade, his kindness and concern extended into that school year. My assault happened near the Christmas of my 6th-grade year. My parents, knowing I would likely need support, shared the incident with the school administrators, and they shared it with the teaching team, of which I think Mr. Eaton was a part. Even after being hurt by a man, I needed Mr. Eaton in my life. He was a picture of what it looked like to love well. I wasn't a Christian then. I didn't know anything about Jesus. And I had no idea if Mr. Eaton was a Christian. I met him before I felt unlovable, and before I ever questioned how God could love me. But I always tried to hold out hope that a love like the church talked about was possible. My hope was, in part, because of Mr. Eaton's extraordinary ability to pour out love in a way that made people feel seen. Even though I didn't realize it until recently, over the couple of decades that I wrestled with that inconsistency, Mr. Eaton's ability to love well would end up being critical to understanding God's love.

I'm not suggesting, not even a little, that people who aren't Christian aren't capable of love. I've known many people who don't profess to follow Jesus and who still love people well. And I'm not just talking about them being nice to people. I'm talking about married couples that love each other well, parents who love their children well, and teachers who love their students well, and none of them go to church or call themselves Christian. More than that, I've known people who would and have, sacrificed safety and life for the sake of others. Jesus said, "Greater love has no one than this, that someone lay down his life for his friends."[8] If that is one of the measurements for great love, I know a lot of military men and women and public servants who love greatly.

When it comes to "ordinary" people committing such great acts of love, I side with C.S. Lewis in believing that all love originates from God. In his book, *Mere Christianity*, he makes the point that all goodness comes from God. Specifically, he discusses that there are parts of other religions that are in agreement with Christianity and that God leads people through those agreements because they originate with Him. An example he uses is the Buddhist teaching of mercy. Professor Thero of the University of Kelaniya, Sri Lanka, identifies mercy as compassion and says, "When there is suffering in others, it causes the heart of good men to move, and that is compassion."[9] Doesn't that sound like the main principle in the parable of the Good Samaritan? It should be the same with how we view love. Unfortunately, instead of seeing someone risking their life for another or deep sacrifice to meet another person's need as great acts of love, we re-dub them as heroism.

He First Loved Us

If love is the accurate estimation and adequate supply of another's need, without expectation, don't all altruistic acts meet that definition? The word "love" has become so commonplace in its use that we find great difficulty in identifying and using it in its true form and instead assign other descriptors to it. What if we started viewing someone who stops a mugging as loving first and then heroic?

Yet, even with all those grand displays of great love, it's easy to see that some of the same people often fail to love in the smaller areas of everyday life. I often fail at displaying love when it would be the best response. That makes me think that intense bursts of love are more accessible than the stamina required for every day, every moment expressions of it. Consider that for a moment. If you had to do something extraordinary, say, lift a car, to save your child, you'd attempt it without a thought. But, we regularly struggle with finding the strength necessary to offer daily, more consistent, moments of love. Moments like mustering patience for an irritable toddler who has been whining for the better part of an hour. Or is that just me? Regardless, at the end of the day, you'd still lift the car, and you'd still struggle with the desire to put them back under it once the whining began.

You might be thinking that a parent lifting a car or a military member sacrificing their life for a friend are just extreme extensions of a love they already possess for the person they're saving. Maybe. But, neither of those situations explains altruism between people who don't know each other. Is altruism a love response? If we consider the definition of love we've been using, some would say yes. Is it possible that we're "wired" to respond with love, even toward people whom we've never met? Psychologists have a few different takes on why altruism occurs, ranging from it being an evolutionary biological response to a cognitive or neurological response and even it being a socially taught response. Maybe it's one or all of those. Or, perhaps it's our intrinsic, God imbued image, our essence. Dr. David Rand and Dr. Ziv Epstein seem to think it's instinctive, a natural part of us. In a study they conducted on extreme acts of altruism, they "provided evidence that when extreme altruists explain why they decided to help, the cognitive processes they describe are overwhelming intuitive, automatic, and fast."[10] Although they don't use the words "evolutionary biology," their report infers that idea. So maybe it is biological and instinctive, but perhaps that biology is God-woven.

As with everything else, Adam and Eve's disobedience in the garden fractured our capacity to respond in a God-reflecting and perfectly loving way. But, it didn't leave us completely devoid of the image or ability. Romans

Three Commands

2:14-15 explains it by saying, "For when Gentiles, who do not have the law, by nature do what the law requires, they are a law to themselves, even though they do not have the law. They show that the work of the law is written on their hearts…" Paul is saying that even if we don't know that we know the Law of God, we do what it requires because it is in us to adhere to it; it is instinctual because it is a part of our nature, our essence.

As a reminder, the law Paul is referring to is the two commandments that Jesus identifies to the Pharisee: love God and love your neighbor. Understanding the law and how we've responded to it is one of the primary purposes of this book. He said that "all the Law and the Prophets" depend on these two commands. Jesus was telling them, and us, that all 613 laws and anything the Prophets ever said is all contingent on those two commands. God built The Law on the premise of love. That means that the basis for all we know and do, in Christ, is supposed to be love. Which brings us back to the point that if altruism is instinctual and the acting out of "natural" law, then it's premise is love and thus always originates from God. If that's the case, our ability to love, whether it be our spouse, kids, parent, a friend, or even acts of compassion toward a stranger, originates with God, even if we don't believe in Him.

All that to say: yes, unbelievers are capable of love. Unfortunately, even with our capacity to extend love, Adam and Eve's rejection of their identity in God created a threshold for the degree with which we can offer and extend love. That causes a problem. It is such a problem that our understanding of love is light years away from how God views love. The introduction of unhealthy and hurtful ideas and agendas only compounds the threshold of our ability to love. Things like jealousy, selfishness, arrogance, pride, and offense all cloud and pervert how love should look. And, even when we do manage to creep even slightly closer to God's version of love, we often shadow it by making it conditional. If that's the case, how can we ever hope to experience real and genuinely healthy love? The answer to experiencing it lies in our connectedness to its source. When we become connected to the source of genuine love, then we find ourselves moved to gather with others so that we can express that love. Experiencing God's love happens through connectedness.

EXPERIENCING GOD'S LOVE

Whenever I talk about experiencing God's love, I always land on the idea that if you've ever really and legitimately experienced His love, then it's something from which you can't simply walk away. God's love causes you to want to abide or remain in Him. It's that attractive and compelling. I'm not saying this to suggest that you wouldn't or shouldn't walk away from some institutional or organizational settings of the church; that's an altogether different thing. I'm talking about walking away from Jesus himself. Love experienced in and through Jesus draws and beckons you to stay and love Him, even when it would be easier to walk away.

Through Jesus

Yes, you read that correctly, "…even when it would be easier to walk away." All relationships are hard. And sometimes, if even for a moment, you have the thought that it'd be easier just to call it quits, just give it up, but you don't. You stay. You stay because of love, and not because you necessarily feel "in love" with the person, but rather because you've experienced genuine love with that person. It's a love that has settled deeply into you, like flames into the middle of coal. Please understand that feeling like it's easier to leave isn't the same as actually leaving. Sometimes you just feel tired and have a fleeting thought that it'd be easier if you didn't have to do "this" anymore. Or is that just me? Fortunately, when I feel that way in my relationship with Jesus, I get to lean into His promise that He'll give rest to the weary and heavy laden.[11]

You might be asking, "But, how?" How can someone get to that level of connectedness with God? The standard, and always correct, answer in a church is, "Jesus." Maybe you just thought, "Really? You're going to go with 'Jesus is the answer'?" Perhaps "Jesus is the answer" seems like the easy way out of actually answering the question, but in many cases, and especially in this one, it is the most sincere answer. In John 17, we find one of the longest prayers that Jesus prayed. Toward the end of that prayer, He prays for all believers and says, "I am in them and You are in Me. May they be made completely one, so the world may know You have sent Me and have loved them as You have loved Me." Jesus is asking God to help us to remain, not only connected to Him, but also profoundly entwined, or entangled, with Him. He's talking about an entanglement that is the same as a husband and wife are with each other. Jesus says it that way so that we know how we are supposed to position ourselves to best identify with the Father's love. And not just that we know the Father's love, but that we identify with it in the same way that He does. Think for a second about what Jesus is asking. No, really. I'll wait.

...

...

...

God the Son wants us to know and receive the same love that He does from God the Father. Understanding that desire, even just a little, should give us a whole new appreciation for what it means to be a son or daughter of The King. The first way we experience God's love is through Jesus.

Knowing God's love, through Jesus, starts with your confession of Jesus as Messiah (also read Savior).[12] If you are interested in how it all fits together and how God's command to believe in Jesus[13] is the first of the New Covenant, then seriously, read Gaylord Enns' book Love Revolution. He does a great job of working out how God's command to "believe in the One He has sent"[14] and Jesus' command to "love each other"[15] are the New Covenant parallel commandments to the Old Covenant ones, "love God" and "love your neighbor." I'm assuming that if you're reading this, you're a Christian and following the command to believe in Jesus. I intend to encourage us, as a unified body, to embrace and obey His New Command, to love each other.

When it comes to experiencing God's love through Jesus, it's mainly about two things: proximity and time. Proximity is about nearness. The closer you are to something physically, the better you're able to experience it. That goes for anything. In this case, we're talking about how near to God we place ourselves. I know this can seem like a difficult thing to understand, after all, how can we put ourselves "near" someone invisible. Jesus ended His prayer in John 17 by saying, "I made Your name known to them and will make it known, so the love You have loved Me with may be in them and I may be in them."[16] Jesus is reiterating that He has introduced us to the reality of who God is, the invisible image of God made visible in Him.[17] Attached to that, He's asking God to help us experience the same love from the Father as He does. Jesus, in us, is what allows us to be near to the Father. Specifically, because Jesus resides in all believers when we are with other Christians, we are with Him and can be close to the Father. Then, in being close to God, He continually pours His essence into us and makes us look more like the Son, which in turn causes us to remain more deeply in Him. This cycle perpetuates in every believer, which draws us ever closer to God, both individually and collectively. It's a happy little cycle.

Time is also a factor in this process. And I'm not just talking about time span, but also time spent. While it is true that being made new, sanctification, and building a relationship takes a lifetime, I'm mostly talking about the investment of your time. It's easy to say that you're "working on" a particular behavior that isn't Christ-like. We do it all the time; "Jesus is working that out in my heart" is a common Christian euphemism for, "I'm still doing that thing that isn't good for me and probably isn't good for others around me, but eventually I might stop." If we're honest with ourselves, usually what we mean is that we haven't put real thought or work into changing the behavior, but we figure that eventually, God will magically take care of it. Ultimately, it lets us off the hook for taking responsibility for that particular behavior. What's not so easy is investing the time needed to change that behavior, mostly because it costs us something. We've discussed behavior modification gospel and its dangers, but following Jesus doesn't eliminate us from our responsibility of participating in the work required for our transformation. We also do this when it comes to building our relationship with Jesus. We hope that if we say "it's not about religion, it's about a relationship" enough times, some miracle will happen, and we'll instantly be closer to Jesus. Maybe we hope others will believe that we're committed to building a relationship, while secretly hoping that it'll just happen.

Even if we don't spend "enough" time actively working on growing a deeper relationship with Jesus, many of us still want to. If we're going to experience God's love through Jesus, we have to figure out how to be close to Him in proximity and time. Because it can seem abstract, I want to take care to address the practicality of experiencing God's love through Jesus. I was listening to a podcast the other day of an interview with pastor and author, John Mark Comer. He was talking about his new book, *The Ruthless Elimination of Hurry*. The main focus of the discussion was Cromer explaining what it takes for us to look more like Jesus and grow in our life with God. To answer it, he quotes theologian, Dallas Willard's answer to John Ortberg. Willard told Ortberg, "You must ruthlessly eliminate hurry from your life, for hurry is the great enemy of spiritual life in our world today." As I listened to him say those words, it immediately resonated with me, as being what was necessary to not only look more like Jesus but to experience God through Him.

The point that Willard was making is that slowing down the rhythm of life, in a way that more closely resembles that of Jesus, is the key to being close to God. Comer noted Jesus' intentional emphasis on living an unhurried life and points out that there was nothing theologically profound about it. He reminds us that this wasn't some "great" teaching, but rather a consistent reflection of Jesus choosing to live a life that was intentional and purposed. Through that, Jesus invites us to follow Him in that slow walk. As part of the conversation, Cromer mentions Jesus saying, "Come to Me, all of you who are weary and burdened, and I will give you rest. All of you, take up My yoke and learn from Me, because I am gentle and humble in heart, and you will find rest for yourselves. For My yoke is easy and My burden is light."[18] He points out that many scholars and theologians propose that the "yoke" Jesus is talking about is likely the Sermon on the Mount found in Matthew 5 through 7.

Comer's argument is that taken on its own, the requirements and actions Jesus identifies in the Sermon are too heavy a burden for a regular person to accomplish. But, when Jesus says come to Him, and He'll give rest, He is highlighting the importance of living every aspect of our lives the same way He does. In doing so, we are transformed into His likeness and equipped to do His good work. Essentially, when our focus is becoming more like Jesus, literally living like Him, the good fruit of that becomes the good works he mentions in His sermon.

I think this also applies to experiencing God's love in the same way that Jesus did. If our focus is literally to imitate the life of Jesus, just as good works is fruit, experiencing God's love toward Christ is fruit. It's the way that we stop trying to earn God's love and simply receive it knowing that it was always there. With that said, becoming like Jesus, imitating His ways, isn't exactly easy. The good news is, there are things we can do to place us in proximity to Him and allows us to dedicate the time needed for it.

Through Disciplines

This next part will be hard for some people to read. So many Christians, myself included, say and teach that Christianity is about a relationship, not religion. That mentality sprang out of how "religious" people have made Christianity about rules and behaviors. It's the same thing that the Pharisees did to Judaism. It's become a performance-based religion, complete with the doctrine of behavior modification at its core. I became aware of it in the late 1980s and early 1990s, but it's been that way for a long, long time.

Because of that, we often place the idea of spiritual disciplines into the realm of performance and dismiss their importance as they apply to growing in our relationship with God. And I've been there; not so long ago, so I completely understand the resistance to them. I believed that becoming too focused on bible reading, spending too much time in silence and solitude, or making a habit out of fasting would translate into me focusing too much on performance, rather than relationship. For me, that mentality even made it easier to justify not having a regular praying routine. Inevitably I'd feel bad that I was neglecting important aspects of being a Christian and swing the other way in my application of spiritual disciplines by becoming exceedingly strict in my adherence to them in an attempt to prove my devotion to God.

Spiritual disciplines are important because of what they foster. There's some excellent teaching around their importance, but at the end of the day, they're about time. When we participate in spiritual disciplines, we are practicing and becoming proficient in our relationship with God. We are putting in the time to cultivate healthy habits that contribute to our relational growth. The more time we spend practicing these routines, or habits, or disciplines, the more time we are placing ourselves in proximity to God. Time spent together builds relationships. If we want to get better at something, we know that we have to spend time doing it. We do this in every other area of our life, whether it's training at work, training in the gym, or practicing a hobby, but for some reason, when we often view this mentality as a bad thing when it comes to our relationships. Marriage conferences are good, but we typically leave the tools we receive at the door of the conference center. Often, marriage counseling is only considered as a last straw, and never a good thing. But relationships are the one area that we need to put in the time to build and grow. I once heard a speaker say that our spouse is not a good book that we read through once and never pick up again. Instead, we ought to view our spouse as an instrument, say a violin, that we seek to master over our entire life so that we might make beautiful music together. It's the same with God and spiritual disciplines.

There are several great books and websites on spiritual disciplines, but some of the more common practices are: silence, solitude, prayer, fasting, confession, gratitude, celebration, and fellowship. If spiritual disciplines are about time, then it is fellowship with others that puts us in proximity to God and experiencing His love.

Through Other Christians

My first marriage was a disaster. We never trusted each other, we never communicated well, there was rampant infidelity, and we were never on the same page about almost anything. When it all finally crumbled, I spent a lot of time leading up to and after the divorce, trying to figure out why and where it all went wrong. As I was starting my journey of really trying to follow Jesus, I set out to pinpoint the marriage failure because I didn't want to repeat the same mistakes. The fact is there were a lot of obvious reasons as to why it failed. The infidelity and not communicating were the primary contributing factors. But those things were symptoms of something deeper, and that's what I needed to identify and let God draw out. As I explored my failed marriage, one word kept coming up and echoing in my head as the primary cause, selfishness.

Selfishness was there from the very beginning. And though it was heavily present on both sides, I could only account and answer for mine. After the divorce finalized, there were several occasions in which I'd be talking with someone about it, and they would ask, "Did you really love her?" To me, the answer seemed obvious, "Of course I loved her. We were married for 12 years." But, the more I thought about the question and processed through it, the truth of my selfishness became more and more evident. I eventually realized that although I had loved her, I never loved her more than I loved myself. I realized that it was that mindset which corrupted our entire relationship. We both loved ourselves more than we loved the other. Because of that, there was very little, if anything, to keep us connected. It's because we carry that mindset in many of our relationships that they fail. We even have that mindset in our relationships with others in the Church and with Jesus.

The scripture that we've been working through (1 John 4:7), opens with John imploring the readers to "love one another." After John repeats Jesus' command, he goes on to talk about love being the primary element for knowing and remaining in God. He makes a bold and honestly challenging to swallow, statement in which he tells us that someone who doesn't love their brother doesn't even know God. Think about what he's saying. If you don't love other Christians, then you don't know God. That's heavy. Unfortunately, I've seen feuds and arguments between Christians that do not look like love, and based on what John is suggesting, it worries me.

As that passage of scripture continues, John explains that God's love for us is best seen and understood in Jesus' willingness, through His work on the cross, to gain God's favor for us. John ultimately brings it all back around to the point that if God loves us in a self-sacrificing (read unselfish) way, then we must also love each other in this same way. This is how we experience God's love concerning proximity. Through loving each other with the same unselfish, other-oriented love that God has for us, we can know and experience God's love. It is how we remain in His love as a body of believers. And really, *that* is the key to experiencing God's love through Jesus: our obedience to the New Command, to love each other.

He First Loved Us

Part Two

WHO DO YOU LOVE

IF YOU TAKE A MOMENT to look around the landscape of modern Christian church culture, one of the main things you'll see is some version of the call to obey the Greatest Commandments; to love the Lord your God and love your neighbor as yourself. You can read it in church mission statements, on their signage, bumper stickers, t-shirts, and videos. All of these mediums declare the call to "Love God and Love Others." Of course, these commands are important; Jesus affirmed that, but it can be misleading in what it means to live as New Covenant citizens. We think that because Jesus named them as the two Greatest Commands that they must be the ones that He commissioned us to follow. That they are the commands that we are to give our focus when learning what it means to obey in practice. I'm not saying that we shouldn't follow them. Surely we are supposed to love God and love our neighbor. There's no way I could ever attempt to argue the opposing view; I'd lose just based on Jesus' words alone.

What I am suggesting is that we miss something important when we begin following Christ with the intent of learning to be obedient to those two commands. The Israelites weren't able to keep those commands, and they recited them as part of daily prayer,[1] in which they prayed at least every morning and evening, if not more. When Jesus came and fulfilled the Old Covenant, it became something that we could experience as a benefit of living in the New. God knew that if we were to understand His intense love for us, He would have to fulfill the requirements of the Law, and doing so would require a New Covenant built on a New Command.

Learning to obey Jesus' New Command, to love each other, naturally leads to experiencing the joy of the Greatest Command, to love God with all that we are, and, in turn, equips us to love our neighbors as ourselves.

Who Do You Love

4

A NEW WAY TO LOVE

A New Commandment I give to you, that you love one another: just as I have loved you, you also are to love one another.
~ John 13:34 ~

A COUPLE OF YEARS AGO, I was out with a friend, and I shared my idea of the new process Jesus is calling His followers to live out. I mentioned the New Command, and he responded, "It wasn't actually a New Command, because Jews were expected to love each other already." At first, he caught me off guard, because my friend is a messianic Christian, which means, in the simplest of ways, that they place heavy emphasis on continuing to adhere to the Old Testament Law while following Jesus. I've been to seminary, so I thought I should have some basic understanding of the law, but knowing that about him, my only argument at that moment was, "Yeah, but Jesus said it was new."

On the surface, "because Jesus said so" is a good starting point for an argument. But, context also matters. After that conversation, I needed to know if Jesus meant "new." And "new" as in, "had not existed before." If He didn't mean it that way, it kind of undid the whole process, and I was back to square one with this whole love and community idea. What I found, as an answer to this statement, and my question was a "yes, no, yes" answer. Yes, from the very beginning, God expected His people to love each other. No, they didn't get it or do it well or even make it a point to include in their laws, and yes, Jesus meant new as in *"had not before existed."*

When God gave Moses the original Law, the 10 Commandments, he was giving the Israelites the answers for loving Him and loving other people, both fellow Israelites, and their non-Israelite neighbors. That's why when Jesus answers the Pharisee in Matthew 22, regarding the Greatest Command, He says love God, which is summed up in commandments 1-5 and love your neighbor, which is summed up in commandments 6-10. So, yes, God intended them to love each other. It'd be silly to think God wanted them to love neighbors who weren't Jewish, but not each other.

But, as we can read anywhere in the Bible, the Israelites had a hard time doing what God wanted them to do. You might say in practical terms that they missed the mark when it came to their fellow Israelites. When Jesus said, "love your neighbor as yourself," He's quoting Leviticus 19:18. That passage says those exact words. Later in verse 34, it reiterates the sentiment when talking about the foreigner in Israel. The word *neighbor*, in that passage, can mean a couple of different things. It could mean friend, which, if taken literally, would let someone off the hook if a fellow Israelite did not consider someone a close personal acquaintance. It was also used in a reciprocal sense, meaning both people involved felt the same way about the relationship and would do or give similar things to each other. It describes a situation in which both parties benefit. If that didn't apply to a relationship with a particular Israelite, then they didn't need to be considered your neighbor. Lastly and more realistically, it did apply to a fellow citizen. Typically it would be reserved for those who were weaker, such as children, the infirmed, and women. In this context, it wouldn't necessarily apply to a non-disabled man who might be an actual and physical neighbor. What it comes down to is that the Israelites had found multiple loopholes for the command to "love your neighbor."

Regardless of God's intention, this strict interpretation of the term neighbor relieved the Israelites of the responsibility from genuinely acting in loving ways toward all people, especially each other. In fact, most other laws about Israelite citizens dealt with how you ought to treat another Israelite person in your behavior, which has little to do with actually loving them. If you were to compare Old Testament laws and stories to what 1st Corinthians 13 says that love should look like, you would see glaring inconsistencies. Loving people, in the Old Testament, has primarily to do with how you view them and how that view dictates your treatment of them. Sometimes treating people courteously or politely may look something like love, but basing that treatment on how we view others permits us to change when the circumstances change.

That wasn't what God intended for us. He wanted our interactions with each other to be something that drew people to Him. He desires a people who look different than the world around them. Even though the Israelites had the 10 Commandments, to set them apart, the way they interacted with each other was, in large part, no different than how the Moabites, the Amorites, the Persians, and later the Romans acted toward one another. They were almost indistinguishable in their behavior. So when Jesus came to fulfill the Old Covenant and institute the New Covenant, it had to be one based on a command that communicated God's desire for all humankind to know His love. It had to be a command that made His people visibly different and let others know that they were His. We find this in the New Command.

THE COMMAND OF JESUS

With a little research, you'll find people suggesting that during His three-year ministry, Jesus issued anywhere between 49[1] and 147[2] commands. One website I saw claims that Jesus issued 1,050 commands. ONE THOUSAND AND FIFTY. While that's a considerable variation in number, it ultimately depends on what you consider to be a command and how you categorize them. Regardless of whether you believe it was 49[3] or 147, or even 1,050, those are some lengthy lists. Some of the listed commands are simple enough, like believe in the Gospel message. Others have to do with things like baptism and how we're supposed to pray. Because I try to stay away from swimming in the legalist pool, I cringed when I first saw the compilations of Jesus' commands that other church leaders had put together.

I recoil at the idea that Jesus issued so many commands because it seems like the very reason He often chastised the Pharisee for their excessive and often oppressive legalism. Jesus routinely called out the Pharisees on their pride in their ability to remember and follow all 613 commands. Because of that, it seems unlikely that He would establish His own set of 147 laws for us to follow because it contradicts His words, "My yoke is easy, and My burden is light."[4] That word *easy* means manageable, as in pleasant, and useful in a good way. The word *light*, in this context, means light in weight or not heavy, which is an indication that you can carry it for a long time. Giving another list of rules, as a basis for following Him, would be contrary to what Jesus was trying to lead us to. Apart from affirming the commands of the Law, Jesus only uses the actual word *command*, as a means of instructing us of what we should do in following Him, on one occasion. And, when He does use the word, He personalizes the call to obey it by calling it *His command*.[5]

WE NEEDED NEW

It's important to understand Jesus' New Command first, before diving into the two that he called the greatest. The New Command is the one that Jesus made a point to give directly to His disciples. It was this command that Jesus caveated with an evidential statement, "If you love Me, obey My commands."[6] And it is this command, that I have seen impact the believer's ability to obey the other two.

When Jesus answered the question about which was the Greatest Command, He didn't include a description of what it would look like to be obedient to it. In fact, He answered the question, immediately added the Second Command, and then identified who was meant by "neighbor." It's essential to understand the audience he was addressing and why He gave the answer he did. He was talking to religious leaders and answering a question concerning the most important law in the Old Covenant. In this exchange, the Pharisees knew how Jesus was supposed to respond and were simply trying to trap Him. They, like every other Jew, knew what the greatest command of the law was because they prayed it, in the Shema, multiple times each day. What wasn't expected was Jesus including the Second Command. It's likely what prompted them to ask Him to clarify who their neighbor was.

Jesus' ability to answer their question and move on, without concern for the gravity of the subject, has always intrigued me. No clarification on what it means to love God, but he then spends time clarifying who their neighbor is. I think Jesus' response had mostly to do with the way they, and we place value on specific people groups, but more on that later. When it comes to loving God, I've spent the better part of my 27 years as a Christian trying to figure out what it should look like to love Him practically. There were so many times that I would read that passage of scripture wishing that Jesus had said, "Love the Lord your God with all your heart, soul and mind, by being a good person and baking Him a cake on Sunday. Love Him by not watching too much television or becoming obsessed with any particular hobby. And make sure you read the Bible and pray routinely." That seems silly, but wouldn't some practical list make it easier? Maybe you're thinking, "The 613 laws were the list, and you said it didn't work!" You're probably right about that.

The Israelites likely sought to follow all of those laws because they were trying to love God better. Theologically there's a lot to say about the law and its purpose. Primarily it was used to set the boundaries of the covenant between God and His people. Of course, Paul tells us that the Law reveals

Three Commands

our sin and acts as a teacher that leads us to Christ, but at the most basic level, it was about defining boundaries. That didn't always, and often still doesn't equate to loving God. In fact, the religious leaders did such a poor job fleshing out what it meant to love God through the law that they had become ultra-religious about it. This misunderstanding eventually caused them to become legalistic and irreligious, in that they were no longer in relationship with God in the way that He desired them to be. That's why Jesus told them that all of the law and everything the prophets had said was dependent on two commands. He was telling them that they missed the point and that everything they did should have been a reflection of and evidence for their love for God and neighbor. But instead of letting the law lead them into a relationship, they created and got stuck in that Old Testament cycle.

Some get hung up on Jesus saying, "...the second is like it," in connecting the second command to the first. Jesus placed both commands on equal footing and was explicit in telling us that loving our neighbor is like loving God. Unfortunately, some take that to mean that we love God by loving our neighbor. That view is not wrong per se, it's more backward than anything, but it does create some problems.

Every sermon I've ever heard on Jesus identifying those two commands always tied them together in a way that reversed them. The typical high point of the sermon was that serving our neighbor is how we love them and that loving our neighbor is how we love God. The implication here is that serving our neighbor is the vehicle with which we display our love for God. Then the pastor would make his recruitment pitch and suggest that serving our neighbor can be most easily, if not best, acted out by being participation in the upcoming church outreach event or serving during the Sunday morning service. And while that isn't entirely untrue, in the end, it isn't the best understanding of those two commands and leaves Jesus' New Command entirely out of the picture. This view of the Greatest and Second commands makes serving our neighbor about trying to love God rather than trying to reveal His love to our neighbor. It's backward. In addition to that, I, like many others, found myself tired and burned out from trying to serve my neighbor enough to show God that I loved Him.

Eventually, I found myself just wanting to quit. That isn't to say that pastors were promoting service as the only way we express our love for God. Bible reading, prayer, and small group attendance were also encouraged, but it always seemed serving our neighbor was elevated as the ultimate expression of our love for God. When we get caught in that cycle, we can easily find ourselves running around doing a lot of work, "for the sake of the Gospel," in an attempt to show God how much we love Him. In the end, a lot of people walk away, empty and tired. They may still attend church, but they do it with a cynical heart and never really understand what it means to love God truly. Sadly that isn't what Jesus told us, and I think His intention was much more explicit, far more straightforward, and less tiring than the Old Testament cycle. And that's where the New Command comes in. It was Jesus' delineation between the Old and the New Covenant. It was part of how He said that we'd be different.[7] It was how He fulfilled the Old Covenant and moved us into the New.

FULFILLING THE LAW

It's essential to understand how dramatically Jesus reoriented the view of the law during his ministry. In Matthew 15, he said, "do not think that I have come to abolish the law or the prophets; I have not come to abolish them, but to fulfill them." Jesus is revealing God's original intention for the law when He gave it to us through Moses. Paul tells us that the byproduct of the Law was that we could see our sin and where we fall short, but this was not God's original purpose for it.

Unfortunately, many pastors, myself included, have not helped to lessen the confusion that already exists around understanding the Law and its place in the New Covenant. Because of that confusion and the difficulty that comes with teaching it, it seems like pastors tend to shy away from teaching about it through scripture like Romans 6:14, which says, "you are not under the law, but under Grace." This passage is right, but in developing a sermon out of just it, pastors dismiss the body's need to understand what God intended the Law for and why Jesus fulfilling it is so important. Failure to comprehend this is what allows so many Christians to feel justified in cherry-picking Old Testament laws that they think are important and use them to build their evangelistic platform, i.e., you're committing this sin, so repent and be saved. In 1981 Pastor John Piper preached a great message about why God gave us the Law. In it, he clarifies the different views of the covenants with Abraham, Moses, and Jesus. He said:

> Many Bible teachers will argue that the Mosaic covenant (made with Israel at Mount Sinai) is fundamentally different from the covenant with Abraham (made earlier) and the New Covenant (established at Calvary) under which we live. The difference, they say, is this: in the Abrahamic covenant and New Covenant, salvation is promised

Three Commands

freely to be received by faith apart from works of the law. But under the Mosaic covenant, salvation (or God's blessing) is not offered freely by faith, but instead is offered as a reward for the works of the law. Since only perfect works could merit salvation from a perfectly holy God, and nobody can achieve that, the law simply makes us aware of our sin and misery and pronounces our condemnation. This is probably the most popular view of the Mosaic Law in the church today, and it is wrong. It makes a legalistic Pharisee out of Moses, turns the Torah into the very heresy Paul condemned at Galatia, and (worst of all) it makes God into his own enemy, commanding that people try to merit his blessing (and thus exalt themselves) instead of resting in his all-sufficient mercy (and thus exalt him).

Piper does a fantastic job exploring how we've muddied the view of the Mosaic, or Old, covenant. In his sermon, he gives five points about the purpose of the law and how it's fulfilled. Foundational in this understanding is the truth that the law is that Moses did not receive it as a means for men to work for salvation, as many of today's preachers can make it seem. Instead, God meant the Old Covenant to be a measuring tool for our genuine love for God. It was supposed to mark out our relational growth with and toward God and others.

And while all of that is true, good, and important, it cannot be missed that the law was also a means of delineating separateness from the surrounding culture. The original 10 Commandments were very different from any of the laws of the people who lived near the Israelites. The first command, "to have only one God," was opposed to other cultures, many of which worshipped more than one deity. Many surrounding cultures permitted murder dependent on the situation. For example, a Roman father could murder his family if they angered him. And adultery? It was entirely acceptable, as long as you weren't a woman. When God separated the Israelites from Egypt, He furthered the process by giving them a measuring stick to ensure they continued in their set-apart-ness. This idea and intent is consistent throughout scripture, including Jesus' ministry and teaching.

In John 13:35, after Jesus gives His New Command, He says, "By this all people know you are my disciples, if you have a love for one another." This passage is the setting apart statement of the New Covenant. If the law, or Old Covenant, was given by God as a means of separating His people from the culture around them, then the language that Jesus uses concerning the

New Command is simply a continuation of that and a glaringly obvious part of His fulfillment of the Law. Jesus gave His New Command to complete the setting apart of God's people. Through loving each other, as Christ loves us, so others will know we are set apart as His.

Even if we understand why God gave the law, we cannot miss *how* Jesus fulfilled it. In each circumstance that Jesus, or the Apostles, spoke about fulfilling the law, the resounding feature was love.[8] Love fulfills the law. Before Jesus' arrival, the religious leaders had become experts in the Law. They could quote it verbatim and adhere to it as strictly as possible. They also made sure that others were held accountable for failing to keep it. But what they missed in all of that, the thing that kept them, and others, from experiencing the full joy and delight of God's law, was a lack of love.

There was a lack of love for God, regardless of how often they recited their daily prayer proclaiming that love. There was a lack of love for their neighbor; those outside Judaism were usually deemed low and undeserving. There was also a lack of love for each other; there were distinct class differences between the religious leaders and all others. Hierarchy even existed throughout the social structure. Because of this, relationships between Jewish people were mostly about how they treated each other. Appropriate treatment of another didn't require an expression of love. And we are in danger of the same error. When we look to the Old Testament, without the lens of Christ, who is the literal representation of the Father and *is* Love, we miss the complete revelation of God's law. We miss that His whole law and everything the prophets said[9] should result in loving God, loving our neighbor, and loving each other.

On the contrary, when we view the law through Christ, we no longer reside on the side of the Pharisees, sitting piously high above everyone else. Instead, we get to become one of the 12, living close to our Lord, who teaches us how to love rightly. And its closeness to Him that makes us whole and complete, perfect and fulfilled, just as the Law was through Christ. And it's precisely because we're incapable of willing ourselves into belief and right behavior, that Jesus gave the New Command. I mean, if the Jews weren't capable of adhering to the law and fulfilling the covenant, why are we so prideful to believe we can?

The origin is unclear, there's speculation that it was Albert Einstein, or Max Nardo, or Narcotics Anonymous, but there's a saying that goes, "Insanity is doing the same thing over and over again and expecting a different result." This definition is perfect for explaining the Jew's, and our attempts at following the Law. And again, it isn't that we abandon the law as invalid. It's precisely the reverse, the Jews violated the Old Covenant repeatedly, and Jesus' arrival and crucifixion was God's fulfillment, read the completion of the Old Covenant. With the Old Covenant satisfied, Jesus institutes a New Covenant, a new binding pledge, or promise, for how we would be connected to and interact with God the Father. And at the ground level of this New Covenant is the New Command, to love each other. The New Covenant reframes the Shema and makes it, "Believe in the one whom God sent, Jesus Christ, and love each other, that they might know you are His. In doing so, you can love the Lord your God with all your soul, mind, heart, and strength and love your neighbor as yourself."

THE NEW COVENANT CYCLE

As a reminder, Jesus said, "A New Commandment I give to you, that you love one another: Just as I have loved you, you also are to love one another."[10] With that one sentence, the whole process of relating to God and our neighbor, changed. Here's what the New Covenant Cycle (*Fig. 2*) looks like:

GOD'S LOVE → BELIEF → GATHERED → Love Each Other (NEW COMMAND) → GRACE → Love God (GREATEST COMMAND) → Love Your Neighbor (SECOND COMMAND) → Witness for Him (GREAT INVITATION) → GOD'S LOVE

I think it's worth mentioning that the whole process is significantly shorter and simpler than that of the Old Covenant process. Don't misunderstand me; by simple, I do not mean easy. For sure it isn't easy. That's why we need Jesus and why the Father sent the Holy Spirit, but the process, as a whole, is far less complicated then we tend to make it.

God's Love

This is unchanging. As discussed, He is Love. His love is so alluring; we're drawn to him by it. It's His very essence, the essence through which He interacts with us.

Belief

Culturally speaking, in the Old Testament, belief was a given. Being Jewish and believing in God went together. It was part of the culture to recite the Shema and acknowledge the one, true God. As Jesus began to reveal who He was, unbelief became the thing that exaggerated humanity's separation from God. Here we have God made visible to people, and they couldn't fathom it, so much so that people like the rich young ruler[11] departed from Jesus, sad and grieving, upon hearing what it takes to inherit eternal life. But, belief in this new process is about realizing the truth of God as Love and how He pours that out to us, specifically through Jesus. Belief in this instance is about heart acceptance and mouth confession[12] in Jesus as Lord so that we will be healed and made whole in our reunification with God.

Gathered

Because God's love is a drawing love, those who come to Him in response to it are gathered into a single body of people. His love places us close to others who share in the giving and receiving of it. As gathered people we become more unified as we draw nearer to Him. We'll discuss this further later on.

Love Each Other

This is the New Command. It is how we remain in connection with Christ and are known by others as His. This is the defining difference between the Old Covenant and the New Covenant. Our obedience to this command is evidence of our love for Him and our commitment to a unified body. This, in the simplest of terms, is what makes us different from everybody else, because it binds us to loving brothers and sisters not of our blood, but His.

Love God

This is the Greatest Command. Our highest achievement and most lofty hope is to abide in this. But, for all our good intentions, this is not an easy command to follow. Without Christ, we aren't able. Often the idea of loving God is too abstract to put into action, but that doesn't negate our sincere desire to love Him and be loved by Him. The ability to rest in this command is what our souls long for in this life and the next.

Love Your Neighbors

According to Jesus, this is the second Greatest Command, which He calls similar to the first. For now, our working definition of "neighbor" is anyone who hasn't confessed Jesus. This command can be seen as evidence of our love for God, in that it compels us to love others as a result of a loving relationship with God.

Three Commands

Witness For Him

This isn't really a command, as much as it is an invitation from Jesus to follow Him and tell others about Him while we do so. Being His witness has everything to do with revealing Him to others and nothing to do with pointing out all the wrong things other people might be doing. We're to be a witness to who He is, not how we think others should act. This is an essential part of this new process, because, before Jesus, the Jews weren't very concerned with telling others about God as a means of changing their belief in Him. Instead, they were primarily concerned with following the law and the proper punishment if you failed to do so. It can't be that way for us.

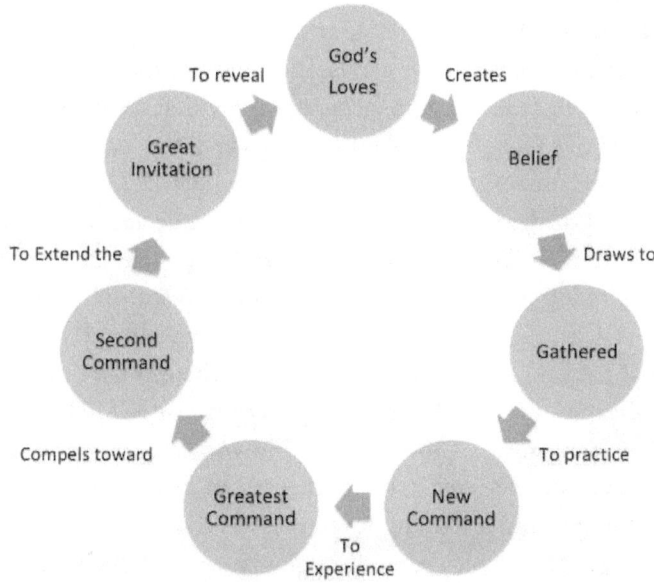

Figure 2, The New Covenant Cycle

THE NEW COVENANT IN ACTION

The new cycle looks like this: just like the old process, it starts with God's love, everything always does. God loves the world. His love draws us to confess our belief in Him through Christ and His work on the cross. God then continues the practice of setting His people apart by gathering us together into one unified body. That unified body begins to build their life together, through the power of the Holy Spirit, in a community where they learn to give and receive love from one another, just as Christ loves them.

A New Way To Love

Because they are obeying Jesus' command "to love each other" they reveal the evidence of their belief in and love for Jesus, who is God. This revealing of our love for God the Son is the practical and outward practice of the Greatest Command. Obedience to the Greatest Command fosters a reciprocal relationship, in which God and His people freely exchange love. Because God's love is all-encompassing and transformative, you begin to love the things that God loves, namely His creation. That love for the people He created in His image, compels you to serve and be with others who don't know Him. This becomes the practical outworking of your obedience to the Second Command, "to love your neighbor." This places you in close proximity to real people so that you can be His witness in the rhythm of real life. Eventually, as His desire to see people reconciled becomes your desire, you become His witness, inviting people into the Kingdom of a Loving King. The process continues like this until He returns.

While this new course seems less complicated than the old, it isn't a more natural way to live. In fact, it's more accurate to say that it's impossible to live this way without the Holy Spirit. And God never intended for us to live in this cycle without Him. We see the evidence for that in the Jew's failure to maintain their end of the Old Covenant. Time and time again, we can see the Jews attempt to live in God's Kingdom and reap the benefits of a covenant with Him while trying to live outside of a relationship with Him. This created a situation in which half of the covenant remained unfulfilled. It was literally a marriage that the spouse refused to live within the established boundaries. There's a lot that can be said about making, keeping, and fulfilling an ancient Israeli covenant, too much to go into here, but you can see God present and establish this covenant in Genesis 15. At the end of that chapter, we see God, as a smoking fire pot and a flaming torch, pass between the divided animals. Typically both parties would pass through the animals, agreeing that the member who breaks the covenant would be made like the split-open animals. God didn't require Abraham to do this. Instead, God took responsibility for both His and the Israelites part of the covenant. When the time came to meet the requirements of the broken covenant, God's love for us, and His commitment to see both sides fulfilled, compelled Him toward that end. This is done through Christ on the cross. In this single act, Jesus both fulfills the old and established the new covenant.

This newly initiated covenant was and continues to be utterly dependent on Him, not requiring us to fulfill any part of it. Even though there isn't anything for us to "do" to enter into this New Covenant, it is established wholly for our benefit. God, through Jesus, provided a way for us to enter

Three Commands

into a relationship with Him without the long list of commands that quickly sprang out of the old covenant. The New Covenant ushers in a new reality that offers us a yoke that is lighter and less burdensome.[13]

Even if its fulfillment isn't dependent on us, our participation in the relationship, like any, does require something from us. It requires two things: 1) That we believe in Jesus as God's Son and Savior of the world and 2) that we love each other, those other Kingdom citizens.[14] These are the two primary commands given as the foundation for the New Covenant. And, while *"love your neighbor"* originally meant everyone, in the giving of this New Covenant, it wouldn't be left to men to figure out and interpret the commands associated with it. Instead, Jesus, Himself, would show us what obedience to this New Command should look like and how it ought to lead us to love our neighbor, those not in the Kingdom, as a means of inviting them into it.

The New Command becomes the crux of our whole connection with God; our ability and willingness to love, in the same way, that He is Love poured out on us. When we begin to embrace the commands of the New Covenant, believe in Jesus and love each other, we get to experience the fulfillment of the Old Covenant. The apostle John said, "If anyone says, 'I love God', yet hates his brother, he is a liar. For the person who does not love his brother, he has seen, cannot love the God he has not seen. And we have this command from Him: the one who loves God must also love his brother."[15] Before we can attend to or experience the other two commands, we have to resolve this essential point. We have to learn to love our brothers and sisters in Christ.

At the end of his video, *Two Roads*, author John Lynch says:

> And I want you to learn to let other people love you, with all of your stuff. And it will free you to love like crazy because you will have experienced being loved.

A New Way To Love

5

THE GREATEST COMMAND

Love the Lord your God with all your heart and with all your soul and with all your mind and with all your strength.
~ *Matthew 22:37* ~

An old saint, being asked whether it is easy or hard to love God, replied: "It is easy to those who do it."
~ *C.S. Lewis* ~

WHEN I WAS GROWING UP, I remember being in church and singing songs about God loving us, but I can only ever remember one song about us loving God. Even today, contemporary Christian music speaks a lot about His love for us, but I have difficulty coming up with songs that are about us loving Him. If we understood what Jesus meant when he says that loving God is the Greatest Command, then shouldn't that be reflected in the language that we use for worship?

I can't speak for the entire church, but for me, the idea of loving God is not an easy one. In fact, it's somewhat abstract as ideas go. There is a difficulty associated with actively loving a God whom we can't see, especially in an internal way. Standing alone, the Greatest Command seems to be one that you might only be able to obey inside your heart. For me, it begs two questions: Who do I believe God is, and what does that mean about who I am.

The Greatest Command

WHO IS GOD?

As I've mentioned, in Judaism, the daily prayer, the Shema, is said multiple times per day. The Shema is one of only two prayers mandated in the Torah or the first five books of the Old Testament. This prayer consists of three primary passages of scripture: Deuteronomy 6:4-9, Deuteronomy 11:13-21, and Numbers 15:37-41.[1] The opens with, "Hear, Israel, the Lord is our God, the Lord is One." A lower tone, spoken response, follows the opening and goes, "Blessed is the name of His glorious kingdom, forever and ever." After this initial declaration and response, the body of the prayer starts with, "And you shall love the Lord your God, with all your heart and with all your soul and with all your might." Does that line sound familiar?

When Jesus answered the Pharisees question, He knew what they were asking Him, and He gave them the correct answer. In doing so, the religious leaders would have known He was reciting the Shema. In asking the question, the Pharisees knew how Jesus needed to answer, and there was only one way He could have. They knew that the Greatest Command pointed to loving the one true God. And yet, they still didn't get what it meant to love God. And if they, the "experts" in the Law, missed it, no wonder it eludes us? If we're honest, most of us wouldn't know how to explain what it means to rightly, let alone tangibly and practically, love God. The truth is that being able to love God is genuinely worked out most fully through obedience to the New Command. However, our willingness and ability to love each other is mostly dependent on who we believe God is.

The different ways we view God, heavily influence whether or not we place someone or something else in God's rightful position, and is called idolatry. Often it is not intentional, but the idol that takes the place of God sets a precedent for how we love Him. Typically the precedent it sets is that you can't and don't love God at all. In speaking of money, for example, Jesus said, "No one can be a slave of two masters, since either he will hate one and love the other or be devoted to one and despise the other."[2] So when an idol takes God's place, you can't love Him, and the idol can never fully offer the type of Love that God is. I say "never fully," because if you place a person in God's place, they may be capable of giving love, but what they offer is only ever a shadow of His love. And it has a threshold. All things and people do. As humans, that typically takes the form of matched efforts. Call it performance-driven love, but the love given is often based on what the recipient has to offer. So the object of desire offers love based on effort and the person desiring love performs, but usually only to the point of acceptance.

Even with our best effort to "give 100%," we can still only give up to the boundary of that threshold. Who we believe God is either restricts us to the threshold or carries us over it. Viewing God as an angry father, a harsh taskmaster, or a merciless judge keeps us stuck just outside of the doorway to His all-encompassing love. However, seeing God as a loving Father, made visible in the person of Christ, allows us to cross the threshold into a world where we recognize Him as just, grace-filled, merciful, forgiving, compassionate, and loving beyond expectation or understanding. This view of God eliminates the threshold.

Without Jesus, we can only operate in love up to our human threshold, and we're incapable of anything else. If we could somehow will ourselves into true selfless love, there'd be no need for Christ. If it were possible, wouldn't more people do it? History seems to reinforce the fact that there exists a threshold for the amount and depth of the love that humans are capable of offering. Surely different people have different limits to their threshold, but it exists nonetheless. Jesus came to usher us across that threshold. It is only in Him that we are capable of a love that truly turns cheeks, blesses enemies, and picks up crosses. When we view God rightly, as a Loving Father and Redeeming King, we get to see real, radical, and reconciling love. Then, through the power of the Holy Spirit, we aspire to that type of love, even though we will likely still fall short. When we receive that kind of love, we desire to reciprocate it back to the source. That's where the New Command becomes the essential component for tangibly and practically loving God.

THEN HOW *DO* YOU LOVE GOD?

As I've already mentioned, the idea of loving God can be abstract. That doesn't mean it's not possible, just that it's often difficult to understand and define. We say things like, "seeing is believing," but as Christians, we are taught to reject that mentality in favor of faith. Unfortunately, because we're human, like the Apostle Thomas, we have doubts.[3] After Jesus' resurrection, the disciples, except for Thomas, were gathered in a house and had already seen Him. When Thomas shows up, the disciples tell him about their encounter, and he refuses to believe it unless he sees it for himself. When Jesus shows up and proves it to him, Thomas finally believes. Jesus' response to him is, "Blessed is he who doesn't see, yet still believes."[4]

The Greatest Command

It's in our nature to doubt and question; it's been there since the Garden of Eden. Often we're led to believe that once we make the leap from unbelief to belief in Jesus, everything else will be easy. Unfortunately, once we become a Christian and begin to realize that everything has not automatically become better, we're too afraid to talk about it. That's part of the point of this book; to talk about the things in Christianity that are difficult. For me, and so many I know, loving God has been one of those things.

As I've grown up in Christianity, how much time I spent, and my desire to spend with God has been the measuring stick for my love for Him. Usually, time spent with God involved reading my Bible and praying. And their effectiveness was often measured by whether they produced the right behavior. Before I start down that road, let me be clear that reading your Bible and prayer are excellent and beneficial practices. Your heart should eventually move toward loving scripture and spending time in prayer. It is a means of connection to God, so that we may know Him more deeply. However, that's not often the way it's communicated. Not only are new Christians not usually taught about why we read the Bible, but also we neglect to teach them *how* to read and understand the Bible correctly. I know people who have been Christians for 20 plus years and have never actually read the Bible. I'm not sure how that works. The sad part is, many believe that they can still have a loving relationship with God by listening to someone else talk about Him. Because of that, they miss out on the fullness of the relationship that God's word has for them.

We can say the same about prayer. I know people who have been Christians for 10, 20, even 40 years, who don't pray around other people, even their "own" people. Part of that might be the fear of public speaking, but on the whole, I don't think it is. The more significant reason seems to be the worry about what others will think of how they pray. Prayer, as a means of communication with an unseen God, does not come naturally to us. And, when it comes to talking out loud to someone, no one can see, some may question your mental faculties.

On top of that, two millennia of professional prayers, painted with eloquence and polished to perfection, can be intimidating. I've also heard numerous people talk about not being "qualified" to pray out loud in a corporate setting. I often wonder if not feeling publicly qualified causes them to question their "qualification" to pray privately. In private conversations, I've had people share with me that they don't have a private prayer life. One person shared that in more than a decade, they have only ever said two real prayers that weren't ones of desperation.

Three Commands

Leading the new Christian to believe that they just need to read the Bible, pray, and attend church is, at the least, pretty irresponsible. On top of that, it breeds fear of open discussion and impedes honesty, vulnerability, and, eventually, transparency. On the contrary, being honest about not understanding what it means to love God, not knowing how to love Him, and not knowing how to talk to Him, allows Christians to explore what loving God looks like in healthy ways, together, in community.

For me, obeying the command to love God with all my heart, soul, mind, and strength turned into a formulaic process. I spent a lot of time trying to feel love for Him in my heart and soul, trying to think the right things about Him and others, and working to do all of the things that I thought would please Him. Sadly, when I inevitably failed in one or more of those areas, I would simply believe I wasn't good enough and must not be trying hard enough. To make it worse, I couldn't talk with anyone because I was led to believe, intentionally or not, that I must be doing something wrong, lacked faith, or I simply didn't love God enough. And the craziest part was, I didn't know how I was supposed to love God or feel like He loved me.

At 32-years-old, my life was falling apart. I already mentioned my messy divorce, but I can't overstate the level of chaos that was my daily life. It was in the midst of that chaos that I found myself surrounded by people who I could tell loved God. At first, I wasn't sure how I knew it, but I could see and feel something different in the way they interacted with the Father. More than that, it was visible in the way they interacted with each other. They would often say, "Love God and others" in one context or another, and as I became a part of their community, I could see that they did both of these things well. It wasn't that they never messed it up, but instead, knowing they didn't do it perfectly, they kept persisting in their attempts. What drew me in further was that those outside the group noticed their love for God and their neighbor.

It eventually became clear to me, even if not to them, that they weren't directly focused on obeying the commands to love God and their neighbors, regardless of how much they said it. Instead, they were more engaged in learning to love each other; they were learning to obey Jesus' New Command. It was their obedience to the New Command that revealed their desire to obey the command to love the Lord and to love their neighbor. It was Jesus bringing fullness to the Law because of their obedience to loving each other. And, to punctuate this point, this fulfillment wasn't a private affair. It was visible and caused people, at least me, to identify them as having

The Greatest Command

been with Jesus.[5] And that becomes the best way that we can love God, through seeking to love each other.

Jesus told us, "If you love me, then obey my commands."[6] He said this right after giving us the New Command. Jesus was telling us that our obedience to His commands, and remember, He used the word *command* sparingly, was the evidence of our love for Him. And if He is the visual representation of God the Father,[7] then by proxy when we obey His commands, revealing our love for Him, we are obedient to the Greatest Command, to love the Lord our God. The New Command is one of fulfillment. It fulfills the Greatest Command that serves as the foundation of the Old Covenant. Unfortunately, that fulfillment ceases to matters if we don't understand how it translates into practice.

Part of what makes it challenging to know how to obey the Greatest Command is that we often don't understand the different aspects of it. We're told to love God with all of our heart, soul, mind, and strength, but we are not told how to do it. These four dimensions only seem to complicate further the abstract nature of loving a God I can't see. Because of that, it's worth exploring each in more detail.

Heart

When the Israelites receive the Law, the use of the word heart is an important matter. The average Israelite would have known that loving God with all your heart was no flippant thing. The heart was considered the center and the primary seat of all of a person's physical and spiritual life. Thought, emotion, and even volition, your will, were all generally considered to originate from the heart. The ability to know God, feel close to Him, and willingly submit to Him were all functions of the heart. For the Israelites to commit to loving the Lord their God with all their heart, they were saying, in essence, seek to know Him with a deeply felt affection and engage with Him from that mindset. While that still may not clear up with loving God with all your heart looks like, it should communicate the weight of that command.

One of my favorite moments in the Bible occurs after Jesus' resurrection and takes place on a beach between Peter and Jesus. If you're not familiar, in John 21, after Jesus' crucifixion, Peter and a few of the disciples had returned to their previous occupation of fishing. All of a sudden, Jesus shows up on the beach. He prepares a meal of fish, cooked over a charcoal fire, and invites them to eat with Him. Upon realizing it was Jesus, Peter throws himself into the water and swims to shore. When they finish eating, Jesus and Peter go for a walk, and Jesus asks him, "Simon, son of John, do you love me more than

Three Commands

these?" Peter answers, "Yes Lord, you know that I love you. "Two more times, Jesus would ask Peter, and two more times, more desperate after each, Peter would answer, "Yes." A lot is going on in this interaction, but primarily we are witnessing Jesus restore Peter after his pre-crucifixion denial.

Every element of that setting would have echoed the night in which Peter denied Christ. It would've been a similar time of day; the charcoal fire would have created a smell similar to the one that was used for warmth that night. The breaking of bread would have mirrored the Passover meal, and asking Peter three times is connected to his three denials. There's a lot of commentary by biblical scholars and theologians on this passage. It's generally agreed upon that the first time Jesus asks Peter if he loves Him that He includes the phrase "more than these" as a means of provoking Peter into self-reflection. This would allow Peter to choose to refrain from comparing himself to his fellow disciples as a way of measuring his love for Jesus. After the third time, Peter seems to walk in stride with Jesus' intention and appropriately and rightly declares, "Lord, you know everything." After that, there is no need to prolong the conversation. Jesus made His point and restores Peter, offering him the original invitation to "Follow Me!"[8]

All that is important because it points back to the emphasis the Israelites, now Jews, placed on the heart as the center of consideration and contemplation of deep issues, such as loving God. Even still, there is so much more in Jesus and Peter's interaction for us to consider when we talk about loving God with all our heart. When Jesus asked Peter if he loves Him, the word He uses for *love* is the Greek word *agape*. But, Peter used a different Greek word for love in his reply. He used *phileo*. It may not seem like a big deal, but if you understand the nuanced meaning of each, it's enormous.

Agape is a divine love, which originates from God, the idea of love as an essence that we discussed earlier. It is a selfless, generous, and sacrificial love that expresses a deep affection in the form of action. It is a love that moves a person to extend love before all the circumstances of a situation might be known. *Agape* is not a human love, although, as Christians, we aspire to love this way. Instead, it is the kind of love that is necessary for loving your enemy. *Phileo* love, on the other hand, is most accurately defined as brotherly love, or a love defined by closeness to another. It's the kind of love that you think of when in connection to loving a sibling or a dear friend. Most sermons I've heard suggest that Jesus used the word *agape* all three times that He asked the question and that Peter answered the first two times using the word *phileo*, then changed his answer the third time, using the word *agape*. The suggestion here is that Peter caught on to what Jesus was asking, finally

The Greatest Command

understood, and answered with the "right" word the third time. Third time's the charm, right? It seems logical that Peter, like the rest of us, would have finally understood the answer Jesus wanted. Then, with his new understanding, he finally answers correctly. Except, that isn't how it's actually in the text; it occurred the other way around.

After asking twice if Peter loved him unconditionally, with this divinely generous and sacrificial *agape* love, and Peter responding twice that he loved Jesus with the brotherly affection of *phileo* love, it was Jesus who changed His words. The third time Jesus asked Peter if he loved him, He asked, "Do you *phileo* me?" Only then comes Peter's most desperate answer, "Lord, you know everything; you know that I love (*phileo*) you." There could be any number of reasons why Jesus changed which word He used, but I think it points to the beauty of an essential truth of Christ. Jesus will, and does, fully meet us wherever we find ourselves in life. He allows us to give only what we're capable of giving at that time, all the while inviting us to "follow Him" as He leads us toward more. There's comfort in that. There's rest in that. And for Peter, after such a devastating event as denying Christ, it was merciful for Jesus to allow him to extend the love he was capable of giving. From a human standpoint, it makes sense that Peter's denial would have affected his confidence in how much he loved Jesus.

One of the truths of this interaction is that Jesus doesn't demand that we love Him with *agape* love, especially if we're not ready for it. However, Him asking Peter twice does show that He desires it. And if He does, is it even possible to love Him that way? If so, how do we get there? The answer is in Jesus' response to Peter. All three times that Jesus asked Peter if he loved Him He responded to Peter with "tend my sheep" or "feed my sheep." Jesus points Peter toward caring for and teaching those who would choose to follow Him. It seems like Jesus is communicating two things here. The first points to what our actions will look like if we profess to love Him with *agape*, and the second is how to grow toward loving Him with *agape*.

Both of these have to do with spending time with and serving other believers. What seems clear is that Jesus connected Peter's love for Him with his love for Jesus' body. Jesus is reiterating His command to love each other. This is what John was talking about when he said that you are a liar if you say you love God, but then hate your brother.[9] Jesus was telling Peter if you want to love me with *agape* love, care for those whom I love, teach them to love each other, and me, then you will love me as you and I desire. And do you know what happened? Peter was obedient to Jesus' command. He dedicated the rest of his life to caring for and teaching others what it meant and how to love each other and Jesus. His obedience to Jesus' New Command "grew within him the ability to love God with all of his heart, even unto death on a cross, just as his Lord."[10] And obedience to the New Command does the same for our hearts.

Our love for our brothers and sisters in Christ is a direct reflection of the type of love we have for Christ. If I'm honest, it shows me that most often, I have *phileo* love for Jesus. And while that's okay, and Jesus accepts that He still desires for me to love him with *agape* love. That only happens in community with other Christians. And because I desire to love Christ like that, hopefully without the actual physical cross at the end of it, I have to love His bride. What Jesus, and the rest of the Bible, makes clear is that your love and honor of God's people is the best indication of your love and honor for God. Not only that, the Body is the one place that you can practice and learn what it means and looks like to love that way. Loving God with all your heart has everything to do with opening it to those in the Body.

Soul

Loving God with all your soul is a little more complicated of an area to consider. If loving God, when we cannot see Him, is difficult because of the abstract nature of it, then certainly loving Him with all of your *soul* only compounds that complexity. It helps to understand that while the Jewish believe the heart is where we experience and express much of what makes us a person (intellect, emotion, will), the soul is our essence.

Remember, *essence* is our intrinsic nature or the indispensable quality that determines our character. Soul, also translated as breath, is God's breath of life or the thing that animates our bodies. It is the thing that God joined with our physical body and made it alive and what it means to be created in God's image. When God breathed life into us, He was putting into us both His essence and the characteristics that make us, us. He animated our body with life that is Him.

Loving God with all your soul is about loving God with all of who you are. The Jews believe that the soul is the seat of our emotions because our emotions are a part of who we are. So loving God with all our soul includes our emotional responses to God. I've always been an emotional person, but the way that manifested before and after God, it's quite different. Before God, my emotions came out often as anger. During that time, I might've called it passion, but it was anger. There were other emotions, but I think anger was the most frequent and predominate one. After God got a hold of me, I started crying a lot. Not because I'm sad, maybe sometimes, but mostly because I often feel overwhelmed with a lot; joy, amusement, awe, and relief. I also feel more compassionate toward others. To be clear, this was my emotional journey and is not intended to be indicative of how everyone's journey should go. So, while there is an emotional aspect to this, it's far more than that. Loving God with all your soul is manifested in you being you. That means relating and responding to Him with the character, personality, and emotions with which He created you.

Again, living out the New Command, "to love each other," is the best way to see this manifested. If by nature, you're a nurturing person, that character trait is most directly God-honoring when it is directed back to Him through nurturing His body. If you're a steadfast "rock" type person, you show your love for God best when you provide support for His people. Because your soul is who you are, if you're creative, then you create. But you create for the good of others, starting with those in His body. Loving God with all your soul has everything honoring those in His body with who you are.

Mind

To be completely honest, this has been the most challenging area for me, mostly because I can be pretty stubborn. I used to think I was more stubborn than the average person, but looking at social media in the last decade has given me comfort. I now realize that we're all pretty thick-headed when it comes to our own opinions. In the end, that probably won't be good for humanity as a whole, but for now, it's comforting to know that we're all riding the same bus that seems to be careening out of control. As difficult as it may seem, loving God with all our mind is possible, and the Bible says it is.

Romans 12:2 says, "Do not be conformed to this age, but be transformed by the renewing of your mind, so that you may discern what is the good, pleasing, and perfect will of God." The implication here is staggering. The apostle Paul is telling the Christians in Rome that as they renew, or make new again, specifically reorienting our thinking back toward how our mind was originally created to operate, then they will be transformed into the likeness of Jesus. Essentially, as you direct your thinking toward God, you become more like Him, and in doing so can know His will, or mind. As straightforward as that seems, it isn't simple. Pastor John Piper thought it was important enough to write a 260-page book on just loving God with all your mind. I don't presume that I'll cover the complexity of it in a few paragraphs, but I want you to get the gist of what it means.

In his book, *Think*, Piper defines loving God with all your mind by saying, "…our thinking should be wholly engaged to do all we can to awaken and

Three Commands

express the heartfelt fullness of treasuring God above all things." That statement doesn't appear until the second paragraph of Chapter 6. That means he spends the first five chapters talking about how we think and the implications for receiving the Gospel. He does go on to break down that statement but essentially boils it down to the fact that we love God by knowing God. Renewing our mind means that we allow our mind to be taken back to the beginning of creation when God was our full joy. But how does that happen? For sure it's a long process, a lifetime one, but that doesn't mean it's impossible. The Bible also tells us how this happens in Proverbs.

In Proverbs 22:17, Solomon tells us, "Iron sharpens iron, and one man sharpens another." That word, sharpen, in Hebrew, *chadad*, literally means, "to make sharp", but it also means "to become alert or make keen." The implication here is that people cause other people to become more aware and intellectually alert in whatever area they engage in with each other. In the realm of loving God, the more we challenge and engage each other to know Him and draw close to Him, the more we become aware of Him and what it means to love Him. Because God is love, to know Him is to know love, and we are only capable of love because He first loved us.[11]

Loving God always comes back to loving your Christian brother and sister, remember 1 John 4:20. In this area, loving God with all your mind requires that you live in a community of believers that will not only challenge you to think of and pursue God continually but also look to scripture as a way to know Him more. It should be a community that is submitted and surrendered to the movement and guidance of the Holy Spirit in a way that not only instructs but, when necessary, lovingly calls out and corrects those in the body. When that's necessary, it has to happen in a way that the body sees God's love on display. In this way, the community of believers acts as a conduit of God's sanctifying grace to help to make the brother or sister's mind new again. For it is only with a renewed mind that a person is capable, even to the smallest degree, of knowing what it means for God to love him or her and then contemplate and act on reciprocating that kind of love. In this way, loving God with all of your mind has everything to do with allowing those in the body to challenge you toward knowing Him more fully.

Strength

This element of loving God doesn't appear in Matthew 22 but does in Mark 12, Luke 10, and Deuteronomy 6, so it's important to include. Not only that, separate from the other three areas, this one is the easiest to put into actual practice. In fact, when the Jews used this word, *me' ôd*, they were

The Greatest Command

talking about the amount of physical force you put into something, specifically an abundant or exceedingly great amount; they called it "muchness." The intention here speaks loving God, with an abundance of force, in every part of your life. It's what Paul was talking about when he said to the Colossians, "Whatever you do, do it enthusiastically, as something done for the Lord."[12]

I've already shared about how a majority of my Christian walk was performance-based; the more you did, and did well, the more you pleased God. Most of that was about behaving rightly, but the same idea applies to "serving" God. In fact, even though most pastors would never come right out and say it, we equate our willingness to "do," specifically serving God and His church on a Sunday morning, with the amount that we love Him. Our willingness to serve becomes the measuring stick for our devotion to God. And, because the best way to serve God is by serving people, we make service our ultimate goal. I'm not suggesting that service isn't good, it is, but many in the church have made it *the* way to show our love for God and His body. Because of that, it often becomes what many churches attach to your "next steps" after "getting saved."

You'll often hear leaders in the church say that the next step in a new Christian's faith journey is finding a community of people with whom they can serve. They suggest that serving on Sunday mornings is one of the best ways to do that. Maybe some of that is true. Maybe volunteering as a door greeter does connect you to a group of people you can "do life with" and perhaps it helps you grow deeper in your love of God and your neighbor. Unfortunately, I've seen that too many times the opposite has been true. I've seen, time and time again, a new Christian or even just a new member of the church, answer the pastor's "call" to serve on Sunday mornings, making their connection to a "community" of people exclusively reserved to Sunday mornings. The people in that group rarely, if ever, see each other outside of Sunday. Inadvertently, Sunday morning becomes *the* thing that defines Christian community. Eventually, people get burned out, or "feel" called away, and end up leaving that area of service and that group of people. And no one notices because they're too busy "doing the work." The connection within this group is superficial, at best, and leaving the "community" does not draw the same tears the apostle Paul sheds as he departs from those in Ephesus. No wonder we don't understand genuine community.

Even if the person doesn't leave, they quickly become content in their shallow Sunday morning connection to Christ and His bride. The connection to that group remains superficial and becomes an obligation more than anything else. Again, I'm not suggesting people shouldn't serve on Sunday mornings; it's necessary. I serve in multiple areas at my church. What I am suggesting is that we have it backward.

Remember, when Christ said "with all your strength," the word *strength* or *might* means ability or great force. He was saying, "love God with all that you're capable of doing and do it with muchness." That includes and is most clearly displayed in service to others. However, it is less of a *next step* in your faith journey and more of a natural outworking of your obedience to the command to love each other. This aspect of loving God isn't primarily directed toward loving your neighbor, we'll get to that in the next chapter. No, this aspect is about loving God through connection and service to His Body. Remember, obedience to the New Command is evidence of our love for Jesus, who is God the Son, and thus fulfills the command to love your God. What we've gotten wrong has to do with what we've identified as our *next step*. Our next step as new Christians shouldn't be to find a place on Sunday morning to expend the new energy that the Holy Spirit has filled us with. Instead, we ought to be encouraging new believers to join a group of maturing believers and allow that new energy to carry them into discovering deep relationship with God and His Body. I know this puts a lot of responsibility on the new believer, but that's how we've set up institutional church. Ideally, the person should come to know Christ because of a relationship with a Christian friend and are then invited into a faith community. That's an inherent flaw within the institutional church and would take another book to dive into it, but because it's what we have, we need to understand how to practice it within that context.

What if we directed new Christians to become part of a smaller community of believers who love each other and practice it in tangible ways? Maybe then they would begin to experience what it means to love God with all their strength. As John Lynch said, "[they'll] be free to love like crazy, because [they] will have experience being loved." Meaning that as the new Christian sees and experiences other Christians actively loving each other and God, they will learn what it looks like to God and His body. As they practice loving God, through obedience to the New Command, it will bear out of them the desire to serve those they love. That desire becomes manifest in lots of different ways. Sometimes it may look like mowing the lawn of the elderly couple in your smaller community group. Maybe it's taking the single mom grocery shopping every week, or going to one of the community member's kid's football games or dance recitals. Perhaps it does manifests as serving your people coffee or opening the door for them on Sunday mornings.

The Greatest Command

Our *next step* after becoming a new Christian should be learning to love other Christians, not finding a place to serve on Sunday mornings. Our service to those in our community should be sacrificial, mirroring how Christ gave to us. It should practically address the needs of those in your community, reflecting Acts 2:42, in which there was no need among the believers. When we genuinely love another person, we have an intrinsic desire to meet their need. This should be readily evident in every gospel-centered community that exists. Loving God with all your strength has everything to do with learning to love and then sacrificially serving those in His body.

WHO ARE WE?

In the end, loving God with all your mind, heart, soul, and strength is most practically, and fully experienced by living in a love exchanging gospel-centered community. When we commit ourselves to the body of believers to learn to love and be loved, we are honoring and obeying Christ's command to love each other and, thus, loving God. When we do that, the day will eventually come when we feel our heart leap toward wanting to share that love with those outside his body. Knowing what it means to love God is also how we answer the question of who we are related to who we believe God is. What we believe about who God directly influences who we are and what we believe about ourselves. And knowing who we are and extending love to that person is crucial to obedience to the command that Jesus said is like loving God, loving our neighbor. Loving God is what equips us to obey the Second Command.

6

THE SECOND COMMAND

The second is like it: Love your neighbor as yourself.
~ Matthew 22:39 ~

WHEN JESUS ANSWERED THE PHARISEES' QUESTION about the Greatest Command, He answered how they expected Him to, but then throws them a curveball. Jesus' answer is not untypical of how He approaches every opportunity to explain God's word. Instead of giving the exact answer the religious leaders expect, He expands our understanding by not only connecting loving our neighbor and loving God, but making them equal to each other. I need you to pause for just a second and think about the seriousness of Jesus putting loving God and loving our neighbor on the same level. Jesus is telling the Pharisees that loving people is just as important as loving God. And, since we've already talked about loving God, it should be clear just how serious of a statement this would have been for them to hear. Jesus elevates these laws to such a serious degree that He said, "all the law and the prophets depend on these two commands"[1] and "there are no other commands greater than these."[2]

If He's that serious, we need to dig deeper into what that means. For the second command, it would make sense to start with the same question, "Who is our neighbor?"[3] We already briefly talked about the different possibilities of how the Jews would have interpreted the word *neighbor*, so instead, let's look at how Jesus identified our *neighbor*. I know you're asking, "How are we supposed to know what Jesus meant?" He was a doer, so we can learn by looking at what He did. He is the literal word of God, active and living, so we have His actions to help us understand what He intended to communicate about who is our neighbor. It's more of a WDJD, what *did* Jesus do, rather than a WWJD, what *would* Jesus do, technique.

Before we get into who our *neighbor* is, it is essential to remember that this is definitively separate from the New Command, "to love each other." This command, as previously mentioned, most clearly pointed to those you were close to, whether in proximity or affinity and primarily included the foreigner or sojourner. The distinction that Jesus made with issuing the New Command was between followers versus non-followers. The intention in this second command was to introduce the non-follower to Jesus and invite them to follow Him. Everything we do in the Kingdom, loving God, loving each other, and loving our neighbor, is an invitation for others to be reconciled to God. It's all aimed at revealing His love with the hope that others will give into the nudge of the Holy Spirit and follow Him. Loving God and loving each other are indirect invitations that showcase a remarkably different love than the world's version. These loves are supposed to attract others and cause them to inquire about the hope that we have.[4] On the other hand, loving our neighbor is a direct invitation. This command is directed toward intentional interaction, with non-followers, to intersect their life with God's divine love. It is us, as followers of Jesus, intentionally placing ourselves in a position to be His witness to them. It's the answer to Paul's question, "How will they know unless someone tells them?"[5] They come to Him by our feet, our voice, and our love.

A WEDDING FEAST

When we consider our neighbor, the first thing that often comes to mind, as it should, is our physical neighbor, the person living next door. That one is obvious. But the word "neighbor" also includes those close to us in our daily life. Friends, coworkers, the person at the grocery store checkout, other parents dropping off their kids at preschool, etc.--they are all your neighbors.

We get to see this clearly in Jesus' attendance at the wedding in Cana. In John 2:1-12, we can read about Jesus and His mother attending a wedding. Cana was only about 4 miles from Nazareth, so it's likely Jesus and his family were close to the people getting married, at the very least, because weddings were often whole town affairs, they knew them. And, since they did walk four miles, which is the equivalent to driving a few hours, they likely had some connection to this family. Regardless, they went to the wedding, and while there, the hosts ran out of wine for their guests. As a response to this, Jesus' mother comes to Him and laments this party faux pas. Jesus' initial response was to tell His mother it wasn't His time, but she ignores Him and tells the servants to "do whatever He tells you."⁶ I can just imagine Jesus' mom saying, "Oh Jesus, stop being so dramatic. Do the thing with the thing for ya mutha." Jesus' mom knew who her son was and saw an opportunity to attend to another person's need. Granted, she didn't individually do anything, but she sought out the One who could. Jesus' response to His mother's desire to adequately fill another's need was to fill that need. Jesus turned water into wine. And not just wine, according to the Master of the Feast, it was the good wine.

You may be asking, "How does turning water into wine equate to loving your neighbor?" Remember, love, is "the accurate estimate and the adequate supply of another person's need, without expectation." In this scenario, Mary accurately estimated the bridegroom's need for more wine for his guest, lest he is made a fool, and went to the One who could adequately supply for that need and expected nothing in return. See? Love. Sometimes loving our neighbor doesn't immediately look the way we think it should. In this case, loving His neighbor meant those in physical proximity to Jesus. Whether they were relationally (affinity) or physically (proximity) close, Mary seemed to have inside information about the wine shortage.

How this translates to us is this. There are people all around us, in proximity, both relationally and physically, who have needs that we can adequately meet. Often it can be challenging to know what those needs are, but that is easily remedied by observing and being with people. This is where living in community with others comes in. And, while it's easy to define those close to us as a neighbor, what do we do with those who aren't?

YOUR SAMARITAN

During biblical times the Jews and the Samaritans were not friends. Geographically they were located near each other, so technically they were neighbors, but not from a relational standpoint. Jews viewed Samaritans as more low-class than anyone else. The reason for their disdain is irrelevant, but just know that the Jews viewed them as worse than many of their enemies. So it was a critical moment when one of the religious leaders, an "expert in the law,"⁷ asked Jesus about how he could inherit eternal life.

Jesus prompts the religious leader to answer the same way as when asked about the most important command. But this answer wasn't enough for the expert; he needed to know how Jesus identified who his neighbor was. Instead of a straight answer, Jesus tells a parable that we've come to know as the Good Samaritan. If you're not familiar with the story, a Jewish man is traveling on the road and is ambushed and beaten up by bandits. He is robbed and left for dead. As he lay there, half-dead, both a priest and a Levite, both important Jewish men, see him and cross to the other side of the road, leaving him to die. Then a Samaritan, whom the Jews hate, passes by, sees the man, and has compassion for him. The Samaritan not only tends to the man's wounds, but he also takes him to an inn and pays the keeper to take care of him. Then Jesus asks the expert, "who acted as the neighbor?" The expert of the Law rightfully answers, "the one who showed mercy to him." The same formula for love applies here; the Samaritan accurately estimated the man's need and adequately supplied for it, without any expectation. After the expert answered, Jesus tells him to go and do the same. And Jesus didn't just ask him to do it; He did it Himself.

In John 4, we get to see Jesus act out the very thing He shares in the Good Samaritan parable. In this scenario, we see Jesus approach a Samaritan woman, who is drawing water at the city's well. It was early evening, which is important because drawing water was typically done in the morning and served as a social gathering. Drawing water at midday indicates an attempt by the Samaritan woman to avoid other women. This was likely due to some sort of shame on her part. Jesus sees the woman and would know what her being there at midday indicates. Yet, He still approaches her. Not only does He approach her, Jesus asks her for a drink *and* talks with her. This is scandalous. But then again, most of what Jesus does is.

The conversation that Jesus has with this woman is significant. Jesus starts by asking her for a drink, which again is unheard of in that day. And the Samaritan woman calls it out and asks why a Jewish man would ask a Samaritan woman for a drink. Jesus then begins to reveal His knowledge of her need for life-giving water. He offers it to her and confirms her more deep-seated need to be close to God. Jesus meets both of those needs: accurate estimate and adequate supply. He even makes it a point to validate her desire to worship God and provides her a proper view of it. After their interaction, she runs off and tells the whole village. The Bible says that as a result, many came to know Him and believe. Jesus didn't just tell a story about Jews and Samaritans being neighbors; He showed what it looks like in practice. Imagine being His disciples at that moment. Imagine the leap your faith in God would take after the initial shock of it all wore off.

Who are your Samaritans? This is a difficult question because it forces you to consider areas in which you likely act more like a Pharisee than Jesus. It forces you to ask yourself, "Who are the people I think myself better than?"

"Whom might I never interact with?" And "Who would I see on the street, crossover, and walk past?" These are difficult questions for sure, but I'm not the one asking them. Jesus is. Jesus forced the questions when He told that parable and sat with the woman. Does the mercy you show reveal whom you consider a neighbor?

ROMAN SOLDIERS AND RELIGIOUS EXPERTS

The mercy Jesus highlights in the Good Samaritan parable isn't mercy for those people who you consider to be below you. It's also for those who think you're below them. During Jesus' time on earth, He lived among some very real enemies. Some of those enemies were, generally speaking, enemies of the Jewish people, oppressors meant to rule and profit from them; these were the Romans. Some were direct enemies of Jesus, people like King Herod and the Pharisees. And just as with everything else, Jesus had a lot to say on the subject.

One of the most apparent places for us to find Jesus' view on enemies is in Matthew 5:43-44. In this passage, Jesus says, "You have heard it said love your neighbor and hate your enemy, but I say love your enemies and pray for those who oppress you." He tells us to offer the other cheek when slapped,[8] to go the extra mile when forced into a task of subjugation,[9] and to give more to the brother or sister who would drag us into court.[10]

None of these things were easy to hear, let alone do. The Romans were ruthless people. They invented crucifixion as a means of inflicting extreme suffering and humiliation on the person and then displaying it as a warning to others. And they used it freely. They would routinely crucify whole groups of people. In one instance, they crucified a group of 1,000 people and displayed them on the road leading to the city entrance. They whipped people with the lash of nine strips of leather embedded with glass and bone, intended to rip the victim's skin off their body. And aside from all that, they drove many whom they conquered, the Jews included, into poverty through the use of heavy taxation. For Jesus to tell the Jews to love and pray for them was, again, nothing short of scandalous. Yet there He was, identifying them as their neighbor and commanding us, I mean them, to love them.

And He didn't just say it; remember, everything He said He did. There are two really great examples of this. The first is in Luke 7:1-10. In this passage, we see a Roman Centurion, who has heard of Jesus' miracles, send a messenger to ask Jesus to heal one of his servants. This is a commander in the Roman military, duty-bound, and oath-sworn to protect and serve the

The Second Command

Roman empire and Cesar, both as a God and the Emperor, asking a Jewish subject, a carpenter form a nothing town, to heal his servant.

What's more, he asks Jesus to heal his servant by just speaking it aloud. Not only does Jesus do it, but He also commends the man on his faith. Jesus says He's never seen faith comparable to this, even suggesting that some of those, who are sons of Abraham, Isaac, and Jacob, read the Fathers of Judaism, will be cast into outer darkness because of their comparative lack of faith.

So, it stands that this man, who is only in Israel to oppress the Jews, Jesus being one of them, sees Him for who He is. At the least, he recognizes Him as someone who can meet his need, and he goes to Him. For Jesus, this man's declaration of war against Him doesn't matter; it bears no weight on Jesus' decision to meet his need. It serves as an opportunity for Jesus to showcase the love He had been teaching.

Another notable instance of Jesus making His enemies into His neighbors was the Pharisees. And not just the Pharisees as people, but also the Pharisees as an institution. The reason I phrase it that way is the contrast between Nicodemus and Caiaphas. If you're not familiar, Caiaphas was the chief or head Pharisee; he was the one leading the charge for capturing and crucifying Jesus. Nicodemus was the Pharisee who met with Jesus during the night. He's the one who Jesus instructed, "you must be born again,"[11] and who would ultimately help bury Jesus. The distinction here is crucial because Caiaphas saw Jesus as an enemy of the institution and people and thus as both a personal and national enemy. Jesus was a threat to Caiaphas' role in the institution. Nicodemus, on the other hand, was a part of the institution that saw Jesus as an enemy but did not share that as a personal view. However, because he was a part of the institution, he still had to be cautious when meeting with Jesus, hence the nighttime conversation.

All that to say, the Pharisees, as an institution, were an enemy, at least in their view, of Jesus. Regardless of how Jesus viewed it, an enemy is still an enemy. And to be fair, Jesus did call them vipers and whitewashed tombs. He was cursing at them, and it provides a good indication of how Jesus viewed them. Despite all of that, Jesus never lifted His hand against them. You might be thinking that restraining His hand isn't enough of an indicator of love, especially since all this time I've been talking about need fulfillment. And, you'd be right. The need he fulfilled for them is the same that He met for us. Romans 5:10 explains, "while we were still his enemies," God saved and reconciled us to Himself. Their greatest need and ours is restoring our separation from God, and Jesus adequately meets that need.

Three Commands

There is a direct, and personal, correlation between Jesus saying love and pray for your enemies and the Pharisees. Most certainly, the Pharisees, Caiaphas included, would've gone to witness Jesus' crucifixion. As they stood there, they would've heard Jesus say the words, "Father, forgive them for they know not what they do."[12] They would've known that He was praying for them, as they had declared themselves enemies against Him. We take Jesus' prayer on the cross in general terms as we apply it to our salvation. The Pharisees, however, would have received it as wholly personal. In fact, they would have likely seen it as a continuation of His blasphemy; you know with the whole "son of God" shtick that Jesus had going. But even in all that, Jesus accurately assesses their need and adequately supplies it, without expectation. And if loving our enemies isn't hard enough, there's a whole other group of people that Jesus identified, who might be even harder for some of us to love.

THE LOW AND THE LEAST

This last group, who Jesus considers our neighbors, is mentioned repeatedly in the New Testament. You might say that how you treat this group is how you are treating Jesus.[13] This is the group that Jesus called the "least of these." In Matthew 25:31-45, Jesus is explaining what will happen when He returns. He's specifically talking about the separating of the *sheep* and the *goats*. Essentially Jesus says that the people of every nation will be present before the throne. While seated on it, He will separate all people into two groups, sheep or those He'll welcome into His Kingdom and goats or those He'll send away from Him. The good news is you don't need to guess what qualifies you for membership in either of the groups; He simply tells us. Of course, belief in and confession of Jesus is the first qualifier, but from verse 35-45 He launches into the criteria for our classification as a sheep or a goat.

Here are the qualifications:
- Feed the hungry
- Give drink to the thirsty
- Talk to the stranger
- Clothe the naked
- Care for the sick
- Visit those in prison

How did you do? Are you a sheep or a goat?

Jesus said that the sheep are the ones that saw Him in those states and gave freely to Him. With that, the "sheep" ask, "When did we ever see you like that?" Jesus answers, "I assure you: whatever you did for one of the least of these brothers of Mine, you did for Me." I don't want us to miss the fact that Jesus called these "least" His brothers. Jesus identifies with the hungry, thirsty, naked, imprisoned, sick, and the stranger, read foreigner.

After addressing His sheep, He turns to the goats and goes over the same list, pointing out how they refused to help Him. Of course, they have a similar answer, "When did we see you like that and not help?!" I can imagine the crowd's disbelief, "What?! We would've never treated *You* like that! If we had seen You like that, we would've surely helped You!" And then He hits them with the same bomb of an answer that He gave the sheep. "Whenever you saw the least of my brothers in that state and did nothing, you were doing it to me. You were rejecting me." Then Jesus sends them away, but not just away, He sends them into eternal punishment.

Jesus is clear on the point that those whom we would deem low and least are not just our neighbors. He calls them His brothers and sisters, so by proxy, they're our family as well. And again, Jesus demonstrated this over and over. He fed thousands, healed the sick, and continually gave to the poor, because it's who He is and what He does. And the biggest indictment around how you serve or fail to serve, the outsider, the low, and the least is whether Jesus knows you or not. The One you have sought to serve with all of your "ministry" efforts may not even know you. Let that sink in. Maybe we should take who He identifies as our neighbor very seriously, and recognize that He calls us to serve them as brother and sister. But, before we can ever do that, we have to figure out what it means to love ourselves.

AS YOURSELF

Knowing who your neighbor is, while important, doesn't matter unless you know *how* you're supposed to love that person. So, how *are* we supposed to love our neighbor? Jesus makes it clear in His answer to the Pharisee; you are to love your neighbor as yourself. That's it; you're supposed to love your neighbor the same way and amount that you would love yourself. The measure for neighborly love is self-love. That means all you need to do now is figure out how to love yourself more, and then you'll know how to love your neighbor. Eh, not really. It isn't that easy. If you've ever struggled with self-image, or self-care, or self-esteem, or self anything, you know that it's a little more complicated than that.

Three Commands

You Are Loved

The Bible says very little about self-love. Honestly, it almost says nothing. The only time the Bible mentions loving yourself is in the context of loving others. One of those times is when Jesus is answering the Pharisees, but even then, He is only reiterating Leviticus 19:18.[14] The other time is in Ephesians 5:23, when Paul tells husbands to love their wives as they love their bodies. Even then, Paul is suggesting that we care for our wives and nurture their growth in Jesus, as Christ does with His bride. But a description of what it means to genuinely love yourself doesn't exist.

Instead, the Bible goes the other way and speaks plenty of self-discipline and self-control[15] and even self-denial.[16] But defining self-love? Nope. And if the Bible doesn't talk about self-love, what could Jesus have meant? As with most of the other things Jesus said, we need to look to the deeper aspects of it. Even though there isn't a specific scripture, we can point to for self-love, what the Bible does speak on is the depth of God's love for you.

At this point, it would be easy to point to John 3:16 for evidence about how much God loves you. It'd be easy because it's true. God does love the world. He gave Jesus as a means of revealing His love and for our reunification with Him. This is literally the greatest act of love that has or will ever be conceived.

But there are so many more verses, in addition to John 3:16, that communicate God's love for us. God's love for us is made clear throughout the Bible. Romans 8:37 reminds us that we are more than conquerors through God, "who loves us." Romans 5:8 tells us that God showed His love for us through Jesus dying for us while we were still sinners. 1 John 3:1 tells us that because of His love for us, we are children of God. There are so many more passages that express His abounding and enduring love. And for all those verses, my favorite and easily the most expansive, and the passage upon which this whole book is based, is John 15:9-17.

In this passage of scripture, Jesus is explaining His commands, and all of them have to do with love. He talks about the love of God for Him, His love for the Father, His love for us, God's love for us, and our love for each other. This passage of scripture ties together what it looks like to love yourself. In verses 9 and 10, Jesus explains that the love exchanged between Him and the Father is a picture of the love we exchange with God. He tells us that He extends to us the love of the Father and extols us to remain and endure in His love. The Message translation reads, "Remain at home in My love," and the Passion translation reads, "Continually let my love nourish your hearts." The key here is that Jesus is explaining what our connection to

The Second Command

God should be. He is telling us that remaining connected to the Father has everything to do with us, realizing the real depth of how loved we are and then living inside of that reality. To be clear, He does qualify it by saying that we'll remain in his love if we keep His commands. A lot of people get bent out of shape about this because it seems like Jesus is placing conditions on God's unconditional love.

While the Bible says God freely gives His love, it never describes it as unconditional. In actuality, there are conditions put on the followers of God; to include how to remain in His love. That doesn't mean we need to earn His love, just that there are actions that are reflective of us residing in His love. The whole Old Testament law is a collection of conditions for remaining as God's people. Violating those conditions doesn't mean He doesn't love us, but rather that we have chosen to depart from residing in His love. The Bible is clear that "God, who is rich in mercy, because of the great love that He had for us, made us alive with the Messiah even though we were dead in trespasses."[17] It's the same with your children, or spouse, or other people whom you love. They may do something that disappoints you or even separates them from you, but you still love them. While He loves freely, our reciprocation of it is evidenced by our willingness to commit to specific actions or conditions. And it's more about compulsion than willingness, although willingness is still necessary. For example, when my wife and I first started dating, I willingly refrained from talking to and dating other women, because I was committed to growing our relationship and getting to know her. As we began to fall in love and eventually got married, my willingness eventually gave way to a compulsion toward faithfulness, because of my love for her.

All of that to say that yes, God freely gives His love, no matter the circumstance, but there are requirements for remaining in relationship with Him. It is our commitment to those "conditions," that is the evidence of our love for Him.

It's essential to see the connection between God's love and what "as yourself" means. In John 15:11, Jesus says, "I have spoken these things to you so that My joy may be in you and your joy may be complete." This verse is a critical one when it comes to the idea of self-love. The word joy doesn't just mean happiness. This distinction is crucial because we often identify the feeling of happiness as a fruit of self-love. Joy can include feeling happy, but it means so much more than that. Merriam-Webster defines *joy* as "an emotion evoked by a sense of well-being." The Greek word for it is *chara*. *Chara* means gladness or expressing pleasure or delight and being made pleased, satisfied, or grateful. Jesus is directing us to remain securely attached to the love of God, so that we will experience His sense of well-being and that our delight, gladness, satisfaction, and sense of well-being will be made whole and complete. Our sense of well-being, our joy, is directly connected to how we view ourselves, how much grace and mercy we extend to ourselves, how much self-compassion we have, and yes, even how much we love ourselves. Self-love in the biblical sense has little to do with an arrogance that falsely elevates your self-importance, and instead, has everything to do with elevating God because you realize and understand how much, and completely, He loves you. That realization leads to another essential aspect of loving your neighbor as yourself; forgiveness.

You Are Forgiven

After my daughter turned four-years-old, she started asking me a question that causes me to pause every time she asked it. I don't remember what happened to cause her to ask, but it was probably something like spilling a drink on the carpet or anything else a clumsy four-year-old might do. My response to whatever happened was to say her name in a startled and frustrated way. While I was expressing my frustration and correcting whatever it was, my daughter lowered her head, frowned, and asked, "Are you mad at me, dada?" It stopped me in my tracks. I moved over to her, grabbed her face in my hands, lifted it to look at me, and said, "I'm not mad at you. I was just frustrated and wasn't thinking about what I was saying." She responded with, "I'm sorry, dada." I said, "I know. It was just an accident. I forgive you, and I always will." I went back to cleaning up her mess as she apologized five more times, and each time I responded, "Baby, I know, and it's okay. I forgive you." By the time I had finally finished, *Sofia the First* had recaptured her attention, so she was finally done apologizing.

This scenario has played out several other times, and each time I reassure her that "she is forgiven," and each time she insists, repeatedly, on reiterating just how sorry she is. Maybe part of it's learned; I think I sometimes over apologize, but I think it's in our broken nature to not believe that *all* is genuinely forgiven. Think with me for a second. How many times have you done something similar in any of your relationships? How many times have you done it with God? Part of why we do it might be because we feel shame and apologizing is a means of expressing that shame and attempting to relinquish ourselves of it. But how much of it might be the difficulty in believing that complete forgiveness is truly available? If we don't believe that we're forgiven, we're likely to view ourselves as unlovable. And, if we see ourselves as unlovable, that will ultimately cause us not to believe that God loves us. That's a dangerous place to be because it impacts our ability to view others as lovable and whether we choose to withhold or extend love to them. This makes understanding and believing that we are forgiven a critical part of loving our neighbor as ourselves.

A few years ago, one of my coworkers stopped by my office and asked if I wanted to grab lunch. I was fasting at the time, so I told him I wasn't eating, but that I'd hang out with him. He asked me if the reason I wasn't eating had to do with a medical appointment. I said no and clarified that it was for religious reasons. He said, "Oh, cool." And walked away. About an hour later, he came back, sat down, and asked why I was fasting. We got to talk about fasting and why Christians do it. As we talked, the conversation turned toward how he grew up in the church, and he shared some deeply personal things. It was a great moment for our friendship. As we talked, the conversation progressed toward the Gospel and what it means for God to extend grace and mercy to us. At one point, I was talking about the expanse of God's forgiveness, and I said something like, "And the best part is that we're forgiven for everything, even things we haven't done yet." My friend stopped me and asked, "Wait, what do you mean? I'm forgiven for stuff tomorrow?" We talked about the cross, the completeness of God's forgiveness, and what it means to walk in that truth. My friend told me that he had never heard that, despite having grown up in the church. He shared that he thought he had to seek forgiveness continually.

Many of us, like my friend, don't know or believe that we're forgiven; and not just forgiven for some of it, but more specifically, wholly forgiven for all things. We assume that it's a continuous process. A few months ago my wife and I were talking and she said, "I stopped asking God for forgiveness a long time ago." I felt like I knew where she was going, but I was absolutely intrigued by what she said, so I asked her to explain it. She said, "God forgave us for everything the first time I confessed my belief in Him and asked for forgiveness. Now it's a matter of confession and apology. I know I'm forgiven, so continuing to ask Him to forgive me would mean that I don't believe He has." She's a smart one. The truth of forgiveness is the belief in the completeness of His extension of it and understanding that it doesn't eliminate the need for confession. We are forgiven all the way, and when we rest in that, we remain in Christ and His love. And that is what equips us to view others as forgivable. Viewing others this way allows us to interact with them in a way that sees past what they've done and into who they are as God's creation. Then we can love them as we love ourselves.

Healthy Spirituality

Understanding and accepting that we are both loved and forgiven aren't separate endeavors. They're actually a part of something larger, called emotional health. As we consider accepting that we are loved and forgiven from a spiritual standpoint, we have to understand how emotional health and spiritual health are connected. Pastor and author Peter Scazzaro explains, "You can be emotionally healthy without spiritual health, but you can't be spiritually healthy without emotional health."

When it comes to spiritual and emotional health, I'm not an expert, although I have been to seminary and am pursuing a license in professional counseling. If you were interested in reading more about both, I would recommend Scazzero's book, *Emotionally Healthy Spirituality*.

In the context of loving your neighbor as yourself, genuinely loving them has everything to do with loving yourself. I know, I just spent the first part of this chapter telling you that the Bible doesn't technically talk a lot about loving yourself. But, I'm convinced that what we think of as self-love has more to do with emotional health. Self-love is about having the right view of yourself. When you know you're lovable and loved, and that you're forgivable and forgiven, you're better able to see yourself just as God does. When you see yourself as God does, then do you see yourself rightly and can see others how God sees them. When we see others as God sees them, then we can love them like God desires them to be loved. Notice how I said, "How God desires them to be loved" and not how they should be loved or how you think you should love them. This command is about loving your neighbor the way that God loves you. In the end, loving your neighbor as yourself is only possible if you understand how much God loves you. It also helps to be involved in a community of people who routinely remind you what that love looks like.

BACK TO COMMUNITY

In chapter 3, we discussed what it means for God to love us, but when we're talking about loving others, how God loves us is an inescapable topic. Everything having to do with our ability to love flows out of Him first loving us. It follows, then, that loving our neighbor requires an understanding of how He actually loves us. This is where community becomes helpful and necessary. I'm talking specifically about *ecclesia*, or the gathered people of God. We've already said it, but it bears repeating, Jesus said people would know we are His by the love we have for each other.

The Second Command

When we begin to consider the role community plays in loving our neighbor, marriage is an outstanding example to consider. In fact, in Ephesians, Paul intentionally uses the language of the Law while talking about the love a husband ought to have for his wife. Just as the Lord directs us to love your neighbor as yourself, Paul charges husbands to love their wives as they love themselves. Paul goes even further and compares it to how Christ loves His church, which is His bride. An important theme in both is that we love those close to us as we would love ourselves. But remember, we define self-love as being emotionally healthy enough to rightly see yourself as God does, so you can see others as He does. And this is where community becomes helpful.

As we gather with other believers, we are joining ourselves to the body and becoming the bride of Christ. In doing so, we are made holy and sacred and set apart for His glory. And what makes us sacred and holy is accepting that we are loved by Him and abiding in that love so that we are capable of extending it to others. And He intends for us to see that in ourselves. It is through Jesus, in the midst of and through His people, that we learn what it means to be loved and lovable and what it means to love others. God's gathered people are essential to the practice of learning and understanding what it means to be loved, so we can understand and are equipped to obey the command to love our neighbor.

THE UNBELIEVER

I need to acknowledge that I know many non-Christians who love people well. They're good husbands and wives, good parents, good friends, employers, bosses, volunteers, and community workers. My intent is never to suggest that non-Christians are not capable of love; they are. What I will suggest is that a person's ability to love regardless of their adherence or non-adherence to the Christian religion is purely from God. Theologian and author C.S. Lewis clarifies this in his book, *Mere Christianity*.

Lewis is answering a question about the contrast between Christian behavior and that of non-Christians. He makes the point that Christianity is about transformation, not behavior modification, which takes time. While answering, he discusses how God impacts people who don't identify as Christians. He says, "There are people in other religions who are being led by God's secret influence to concentrate on those parts of their religion which are in agreement with Christianity, and who do belong to Christ without knowing it." The implication here is that all good qualities and everything praiseworthy come from God.[18] Since God is love, everyone's ability to love originates from God. Those who are submitted to Him become capable of passing the previously mentioned threshold, into the realm of loving like God.

With that said, the point being made is about expectation, not ability. When we commit ourselves to Christian community, with the intention of loving each other, we assume those who are in that community are operating with the same purpose. When we go into our local communities, with the intention to love our neighbor, we shouldn't assume unbelievers are intent on the same purpose. We can find ourselves serving a group of people, who while thankful, aren't capable of reciprocating our love. And we shouldn't expect them to. Remember love is the accurate estimate and the adequate supply of another's need *without* expectation. Our expectation for those identified in the New Command versus the Second Command should be different because each focuses on different groups of people.

Think of it this way. When you participate in your church's outreach project, whatever it is, painting houses, shoveling snow, etc., what do you expect from the people you're serving? If your answer is anything other than "nothing" then check your intention for loving your neighbor. Notice I didn't ask, "What's your hope for the people you're serving?" Expectation and hope are two different things. You should hope that they see God in your love and service. You should hope that they feel drawn to Him. Maybe even hope that they visit your church. But, we don't love with the expectation that any of that happens. And, we certainly don't expect them to love us back in the same way.

We spend time with other Christians, practicing the New Command, so we're filled, to overflowing, with the love of God, to pour it out on and in those who don't yet know Him. When we misplace our expectations, we run the risk of draining ourselves to the point of exhaustion and burn out. Have you ever known someone, maybe you're that someone, who was completely committed to "outreach" and giving and then one day they just quit? They had to "step back" for a "season." Or they just leave church altogether, because they were too tired or burned out to keep coming. What was the issue? Why were they able to just leave? What I would argue as one of the main reasons is the lack of a Christian community that is committed to practicing the New Command. The burned-out person emptied him or herself so much, over and over, and didn't have a community that replenished the love that they so willingly gave away. This happens because while obedience to the New Command fills, obedience to the Second Command primarily empties.

ALL THINGS WORK TOGETHER

When we look at all three of these commands collectively, we should experience the abundance of life that Jesus spoke of in John 10:10. The New Command is intended to draw us into a body of loving people, focused on glorifying Jesus. That, in turn, reveals our love for Jesus, and the Father, resulting in the fulfillment of the Greatest Command. It is only then that we are capable, and even desire, to obey the Second Command, without becoming tired. None of this allows us to sit idle in the Kingdom. All of it should move us toward the ministry of reconciliation. In 2009, author and motivational speaker, *Simon Sinek,* wrote a book titled, *Start with Why*. Since then, he has run an entire business focused on helping people discover why they do what they do, primarily in the area of work and calling. On his website, he has in big, bold letters, "The WHY is the purpose, cause or belief that drives every one of us." This is true about love in the Kingdom. Understanding what love is and whom we're called to love is useless if we don't know why we love. Against Simon's advice, I'm going to end with the why.

Part Three

WHY WE LOVE

WHEN WE CONSIDER WHY this love thing is so important, we need to look at why Jesus came into the world. Most of us know that His purpose is found in John 3:16, which says, "For God loved the world in this way: He gave His one and only Son, so that everyone who believes in Him will not perish, but have eternal life." This is the Good News. But we have to continue reading if you want to understand the fullness of why Jesus came and what He intended when He invited us to participate in the Great Commission. Continuing in John 3:17-21, we see Jesus give a full picture of His purpose. He says:

> For God did not send His Son into the world that He might condemn the world, but that the world might be saved through Him. Anyone who believes in Him is not condemned, but anyone who does not believe is already condemned, because he has not believed in the name of the One and Only Son of God. "This, then, is the judgment: The Light has come into the world, and people loved darkness rather than the Light because their deeds were evil. For everyone who practices wicked things hates the Light and avoids it, so that his deeds may not be exposed. But anyone who lives by the truth comes to the Light, so that his works may be shown to be accomplished by God."

This is so important. Jesus is saying He didn't come to condemn us, but save us through Him. He says He is the Light spoken into the darkness. The Jewish people He was talking to would have understood this as a connection to Genesis 1:3. They would've understood Jesus' implication that God was creating something new through Him. It would have added to the Pharisee's evidence of Him as a blasphemer. In this passage, Jesus is saying His purpose, and by proxy ours, is to reveal the truth so people may come to the

Why We Love

Light, meaning Him. That only happens apart from condemnation. Inviting people into the Light has to happen through love because God is Love.

Out of that purpose, Jesus lived and practiced His true identity; Love. He made it abundantly clear that we are to operate in the same way. That's why He says things like, "Among you it shall be different"[19] when talking about exercising authority and serving each other. He was setting up His Kingdom, and His Kingdom is an upside-down one; leaders serve, and the first is last. And it all starts and ends with a posture of love.

The following chapters are about why we love. The most basic and ultimate reason is discipleship. I know that there are a lot of ideas for what disciple-making looks like, and I would encourage you to find one that is biblical and effective and then implement it. That's not exactly what I want to do with the following chapters.

Instead, I want to approach it from a purposeful position and talk about what community, disciple making, and being his witness means in the context of love. The entire premise of this book is that we must first learn to and then begin to practice loving each other. When we obey the New Command, we learn to obey the Greatest Command and are compelled and equipped to obey the Second Command. Or more simply put, when we love each other, we are expressing our love for God and are more capable of loving our neighbor; and, not without a purpose.

The entire process of learning and expressing God's love moves toward invitation. We go to our neighbors, spurred on by love, to invite them into Kingdom community. They enter into a community of love, where they learn to love and be love, while learning to walk as Christ. In doing so, they experience a genuine love relationship with God that compels them to go to their neighbor with the same purpose for which they were invited. And it's a cycle that continues until Jesus comes. It is the way that we grow His Kingdom and see heaven come to earth. It looks like this:

***

Three Commands

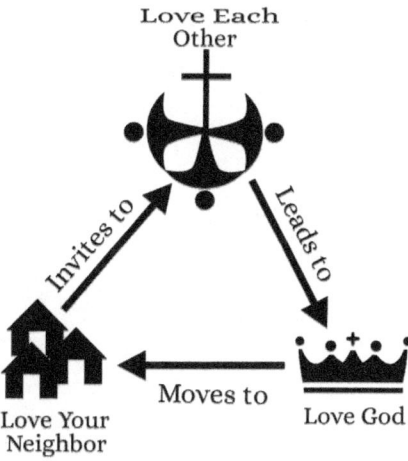

Figure 3, The Commands Fulfilled

If we are to do any of that well, we'll need to understand some basic principles of what discipleship could resemble. These last few chapters will focus on different principles associated with living in a committed Christ-centered community. The intention is to walk through how discipleship flourishes when we first learn to give and receive love so that we're equipped to love others as an invitation into the Kingdom.

As we begin the end, I want us to encourage us to look at the Great Commission in a new way. What if the Great Commission isn't a command? Jesus never called it the Great Commission, we did. What if instead, He intended it to be a direction in which we are to implement the commands He gave us. What if it was an invitation to "come and follow" Him? When we obey His commands to love, it should result in a move toward the Great Commission. Experiencing the love of Him and His Body should cause us to want to tell others about Him, as His witness, so that they may know and follow Him, as His disciples.

Why We Love

7

TO SPUR EACH OTHER ON

And we have this command from Him: The one who loves God must also love his brother.
~ 1 John 4:21 ~

JOHN TELLS US OVER AND OVER that if we do not love our brothers and sisters in Christ, we cannot and do not love God. He says, "If you say you love God, but do not love your brother, then you're a liar."[1] He makes it impossible for someone to disconnect loving God from loving his or her fellow Christian. That means our ability, and on some level desire, to love God depends on our willingness and commitment to loving each other. Notice it has nothing to do with how well we love each other, although we should always strive to love with the same fullness that Jesus did. Our willingness to practice and grow in love is what draws us toward unity and reveals our love for God. That willingness to practice our obedience to the New Command has to happen in community.

Ultimately, community is about connection; connection is about unity; unity is about commitment. Community is a commitment of obedience to Jesus' command to love each other and His invitation to make disciples. And it needs to be accomplished in that order. If not, we are merely asking people to join a program. But, when we focus on loving each other in community, out of reverence for Jesus, then we accelerate the process of being transformed into His likeness. This is not about forcing relationships inside of a system. Relationships should, and indeed do, develop naturally. They have to. Community, however, is built intentionally. It's about intentional commitment to Jesus and His Bride. Gospel-centered community is about relationships with intention. Gospel community is how we learn to be like Jesus because it is the context in which true discipleship happens.

I'm well aware that community has become a church buzzword. I've been reading, talking, and writing about it for long enough to know that the way church folk talk about and participate in community is often two very different things. But remember, this is about willingness to grow in our obedience to love each other. I think it's necessary to understand that our willingness does not automatically equal ability. We can be willing to learn something, but still be bad at it. In the context of loving each other, willingness to grow is about knowing and practicing.

KNOWING AND PRACTICING

I once wrote an article titled *Loved People, Love People*. I bet you can guess the premise of the article. I realize now that that series was just the beginning of the almost seven-year journey toward writing this book. The idea that loved people love people is 100% about knowing and practicing.

When we talk about being loved people, we have no choice but to talk about the Gospel. Remember, our capacity to love our neighbor, as yourself, is wrapped up in your understanding and belief that you are lovable and loved and that you are forgivable and forgiven. Loved people are those who believe and accept the truth that God loves them. That doesn't mean they never struggle or doubt, just that in their heart they know that they are loved. Unfortunately, knowing and believing that He loves you isn't always an easily traveled path. Getting to that place of knowing to belief requires that you experience His love. I know people who have been Christians for 20 years who have never felt His love.

Mother Teresa wrote over 40 letters in which she lamented her inability to feel God close to her. She spoke of fighting off feelings of darkness and torture. She wrote about her struggle with feeling thrown away and being unwanted and unloved by God. In one of her letters to a friend, written in 1979, she said, "Jesus has a very special love for you. As for me, the silence and emptiness is so great that I look and do not see, listen and do not hear. The tongue moves [in prayer] but does not speak." Her faith crisis spanned 40 years. I can't imagine doing the work she did for so long and feeling that way for 40 years. Of course, I don't know why she felt that way, and I can't fathom what caused her to keep going, but I can't help but wonder if it had something to do with a lack of connection to a body of believers who practiced the New Command. I know that she had fellow Sisters and

Three Commands

volunteers who ministered to the poor with her, but I wonder what the ratio was between their focus of obedience to loving their neighbor versus loving each other. If it was grossly imbalanced, I could see how she felt so empty. Because the Word of God, literally Jesus,[2] resides with His people, I wonder if being with a community of people who practice loving each other would have helped Mother Teresa to feel and hear God better. I think that's part of why Jesus gave the New Command; as a way to remedy and lessen the potential for emptiness and burn out.

I've been lucky enough to be a part of at least two communities that have sought and pursued obedience to the New Command. I'm convinced that it was through those two communities that I experienced the genuine love of Christ. That doesn't mean there haven't been times that it felt absent, of course there were. But, in those times of lack, I had a point to reference for how His love should feel. And it was a tangible one. That's what has kept me in His embrace, even when I didn't feel like it. Community helped me to genuinely know His love and believe that I was loved.

Knowing and believing that you are loved should naturally lead you to love others. It is in this that God unifies us into one body, under the Headship of Jesus. God, through Christ, creates everything, even and especially unity of the Body. In realizing this, it is also essential to understand that it takes practice to sustain unity. Surely God, through the Holy Spirit, does maintain our unity, but it still requires us to practice loving each other. For different groups of people practicing this will look different. Because of that, I never want to offer a one-size-fits-all "model" for building community.

Instead, I'd like to offer some principles for living in a committed community with other believers. Remember that community is ultimately about relationships with intention. It requires a commitment from those involved in its practice. If we approach community from a place of commitment to Christ and His Bride, the relationship will flourish. Acts 2:42-47 gives us a set of principles that guide us toward what it looks like to live in a committed community with other Christians. The goal here is not to "go back" to the Acts church, but rather examine what they did and apply it in our current context. The principles we see in the early church create a process that is flexible enough to be implemented under various strategies, in any culture, and at any point in history.

I've seen these principles played out, in one form or another, in multiple communities. They are principles that I, with a small group of friends, have worked through and articulated in a way that, we hope, is clear and simple.

These are also principles that my wife and I are trying to implement and live out with a small group of friends. They are biblically-based principles that focus on Jesus. When a group of Christians commit to and practice them, they can result in a loving community focused on making disciples. My friends and I have come to refer to the whole of these guiding principles as a Gospel Centered Community (GCC), and I'm excited to share it with you.

These guiding principles are crucial to directing us toward becoming a unified body that glorifies Christ. These principles guide us through a set of actions meant to ground us in a deeper relationship with God and each other. The first two guiding principles build us into a GCC, one that reveals Christ and in which we actively participate in mutual discipleship. The third principle is intended to move us into a missional mindset, one focused on the Great Commission. It should spur us on toward being His witnesses and make disciples of all nations. We call this Gospel Centered Missional Community (GCMC).

GOSPEL CENTERED COMMUNITY

GCC is entirely about Jesus. It's about pursuing, praising, and making much of Him through connection with Him and His while practicing His commands. If there is any other underlying motive, if it becomes about you or your people, then it is no longer an authentic Christ-centered community. It is important to note that this type of community is hard, really hard. It moves you from the ease of attending a 90-minute Sunday morning event and requires your whole life. It is messy, consuming, and forces you to abandon many, if not all, of your presuppositions about being the church. It forces you to go to Christ every day, for the sake of and on behalf of the community. It requires that you seek God more deeply and submit in ways that you may have never considered. And because it's hard, it takes time, a lot of time, probably a lifetime.

***

Three Commands

Visually the process looks like this:

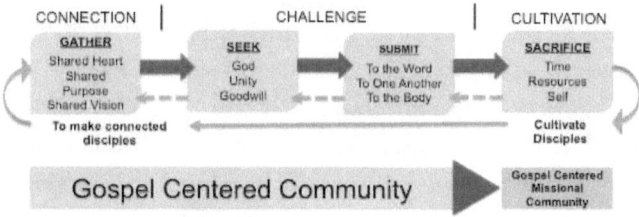

Figure 4, Principles for Living in Committed Community

As I mentioned, the process begins with three guiding principles. Those guiding principles are *Connection, Challenge, and Cultivation*. Each of the guiding principles is held up and advanced toward GCMC by different committed actions. Again, community is relationship with intentional commitment. These *committed actions* are precisely what they sound like; actions that each member of the community commits to in order to see Christ exalted and community flourish under His Headship. Each *committed action* has three elements that are defining characteristics of that action. For example, the commitment to gather is defined by what you gather around. When you gather, you should gather around a *shared heart* for following Jesus, a *shared purpose* of loving each other, God and neighbors, and a *shared vision* to see God's Kingdom come and His will be done on earth.[3] The commitment to gather around those things is what strengthens the community *connection* and advances it toward the *challenge* of discipleship and, ultimately, the mission of *cultivating* disciple-makers.

All three of the guiding principles should unify the community and grow its members into mature disciples of Jesus. We are committing to the following three actions:

- To be connected to other believers.
- To challenge one another to walk like Christ.
- To cultivate disciples who make disciples.

Since this chapter focuses on growing into a community in which members spur each other on to love and good works,[4] we're only going to talk about the first two principles, *Connection, and Challenge*.

CONNECTION TO OTHER BELIEVERS

When we commit to being connected to other believers, we are committing to allow God to draw us together in one body through one hope.[5] This is not a commitment that is entered into blindly. Of course, it may start as a small-group gathering of people who don't know each other, but it should grow to a place where commitment becomes part of the natural progression.

About a million years ago, when I was leading a college ministry, whenever anyone was involved in a dating relationship, the members would always ask the dating couple if they had already had a "DTR" conversation. DTR means "define the relationship." Mainly everyone wanted to know if the dating couple had a clear view and understanding of the commitment and intent of the relationship. That should be the natural progression of any community. At some point, they should seek to define their intention for involvement in the community and what they're willing to commit to the other members. A healthy community starts with the commitment to remain connected to one another.

Connecting Ourselves To Each Other

At its most basic "to connect" simply means to *join* or *unite*. In this context, it does mean that, but it also carries a much deeper meaning. When Christians intentionally commit to being connected, they bind themselves together as one body under the headship of Jesus. They are communicating to each other, and others, their desire for unity with Christ and His Bride. This is about far more than signing a "covenant" or membership application. It's about allowing the Holy Spirit to draw your hearts to one another collectively. It's in this drawing and binding that the practice of loving each other[6] is learned and applied. And, in learning to obey Jesus' New Command, the community is bound ever more tightly together.

Gathered before Scattered

Connection in the context of GCC is about far more than a simple association. We are connected to others in many aspects of our lives. We're connected to people at work, other parents in our children's class, and the barista at our favorite coffee joint. And while these are important relational connections, they do not provide the same intimacy or authenticity as a Christian community. For it to be an authentic Christian community, our connection to other believers has to be focused on unity in Christ. And because it is Christ who gathers us, it is important to know what elements strengthen and uphold our connection to each other. It is those elements that give substance and meaning to our gathering and reveal our commitment to connection.

GCC *Gathers* Around a…

Shared Heart. First and foremost, your shared heart for gathering together should be your desire for and to follow Jesus. This is the core of what draws you together as a community. It is your commitment to Christ and His mission that binds you together as a body. Mutually identifying as citizens of His Kingdom will cause us to desire genuine community and allow God to build us into one. Defining the heart of your community will help anchor you to Christ and each other.

Questions to ask as a community:
- What are we *for* as a group?
- What is our individual and collective nature?
- What of importance lies at the center of our gathering?

Shared Purpose. The primary shared purpose of a maturing community of Saints should be to practice obedience to Jesus' command to love each other. Beyond that primary purpose, different groups will have different purposes. The defining element of shared purpose is meaning.

Questions to ask as a community:
- Beyond loving each other, why do you exist as a community?
- The foundation for your existence as a community is Jesus, but why else?
- Where can you point to meaningful interactions within the gathering?
- What things do you regularly do that provide meaning?
- What do you look forward to when gathering?

- Where might you, as a group, need to grow in meaningful ways?

Shared Vision. As a community, you should share in Jesus' prayer and vision to see God's Kingdom come, and His will be done on earth as it is in heaven. The idea of "vision" might bring with it thoughts of programs and procedures, but it's not about that. Vision is about dreaming. Vision is about allowing the Holy Spirit to capture your mind and lead you into possibility. It's about letting Holy Spirit build in your community a view and understanding of what heaven on earth means and what living in Kingdom culture looks like in practical terms.

Questions to ask as a community:
- What does God desire for us to accomplish as we gather?
- What does growth look like?
- How or even will we multiply?
- What might come next?

A commitment of connection might be verbalized as:

We will connect ourselves to other believers by gathering around a shared heart, purpose, and vision.

Acts 2 and the Commitment to Connection

I want to attach a commitment to connection back to Acts 2. In the following, I italicized the portion of the scripture that is pertinent to that specific commitment.

This entire passage of scripture is replete with the new followers showing a commitment to gather together. In verse 42, we read that they *"devoted themselves to* the apostles' teaching and *the fellowship."* This reveals that the believers were committed to continual communion with each other. This communion wasn't the Sunday morning cracker and thimble of juice event. This communion was about learning and the exchange of affection and joy between the members.

In addition to verse 42, we see verse 44 saying, "And *all who believed were together* and *had all things in common."* In this verse, we see the saint's commitment to maintaining a collective heart and mind as they gather. We can see this type of unified agreement throughout the New Testament.[7] They gathered around a shared heart for Jesus and each other. They shared a purpose for equipping each other to do the work of the ministry[8] and spurring each other on to love and good works.[9]

Lastly, verse 46 tells us, "And *day by day, attending the temple together* and *breaking bread in their homes*, they received their food with glad and generous hearts." The Saints gathered to worship and eat together daily. It was not exclusively about a Sunday or Wednesday gathering. They gathered out of affection for one another, with glad and generous hearts, rather than out of a sense of duty or crossing off a religious checklist item.

These passages of scripture reveal the Christian's commitment to remain connected to one another by gathering for unity. In his commentary, Matthew Henry describes the importance and benefit of their unity by saying, "they were much together." Their connection wasn't just about being with like-minded people and was about far more than mere proximity to a church. Their connection was about being transformed into the likeness of Christ, together. Their commitment to connection also moved them toward challenging each other to walk as Jesus walked.

As these elements encourage a community to uphold their commitment to gathering with each other, it will also move them forward toward a commitment to challenge one another to walk more like Jesus.

CHALLENGE ONE ANOTHER TO WALK AS CHRIST

Challenge is always a tricky thing. We say we want others to challenge us, but I'm not sure we mean it. The myriad of ways by which we have simplified absolutely everything proves this point. And whatever we've figured out how to simplify, we demand that it be made simpler. It wasn't enough to have one device that replaced your telephone, pager, camera, paper notepad, desktop computer, paper maps, then car navigation systems, thermometer, Walkman, paper books, etc. No, we needed to remove the need to type anything physically. We just want to be able to talk into it and have it do whatever the thing is we want done. Look at social media. We want to share our opinion and have it accepted without argument. When someone comes along and challenges it, we get angry that they would dare comment on *my* page. Who do they think they are, making a comment about my opinion that I expressed through sharing an article that I didn't write? We say we want to be challenged, but only in areas that we choose.

To Spur Each Other On

Any good athlete, who wants to be better, looks to be challenged. They push themselves and find people who will push them ever harder in the direction of growth. They seek out bigger and bigger challenges, in hopes that they will be better than they were the day before. Whether we want to win or just know we're good enough, fast enough, strong enough, only then do we welcome others challenging us. It's weird to me that we bristle against that process when it comes to our spiritual growth, but not our physical or intellectual growth. I know there are those whom give their spiritual maturity that level of commitment, but many of us don't. We quote scripture like, "Iron sharpens iron,"[10] but only mean it if it can be said in the context of a weekly bible study that only gives the appearance of being us challenged. When we walk away from the group, the potential for someone to hold me accountable to being sharpened evaporates. That's not to suggest that we don't desire to be challenged, just that we often lack the discipline and humility required of such a commitment. Genuine Jesus-focused community that is focused on Jesus and co-discipleship welcomes this type of challenge.

Within GCC, challenge grows out of love for Jesus and each other and a desire to abide in His love. The word *challenge* has a lot of different definitions, but perhaps the one that fits closest within the context of community is "an invitation to take part in." And what are we taking part in? We are taking part in the activity of growing more fully into the likeness of Jesus. Specifically, it is answering the call to "stir up one another to love and good works"[11] and "encouraging one another" so that we may walk as Jesus walked.[12] And we challenge each other through the actions of seeking and submission.

GCC Communally **Seeks**...

> ***God.*** Seeking God together should be relatively simple for most Christians to understand, even if we don't do it consistently. When we seek to know God, we are better able to see Christ. When we see Christ clearly, we allow His light to shine on the areas of our life where we might fall short of His glory. In identifying those areas, we can present them to God, in repentance, so that we can address them within our community. A community of people who love you will challenge you to seek God, both individually and corporately, continually. How that happens for you and your community is up to you. It may be daily or weekly bible readings, communal and/or private prayer, bible studies, times of silence or solitude, fasting, or all

of it; you guys get to decide that. Whatever you decide, it should be focused on a commitment to challenge each other to seek God with passion and enthusiasm.

Unity. This element is about the harmony of heart and mind, with Christ, as His Body. Unity does not mean agreement on 100% of issues, but rather a joining together in pursuit of Christ, truth, and love for each other. Of course, disagreement will come, so it is essential to decide what issues are "open-handed" and not worth breaking communion over. But, there are, and should be, things that you maintain "the unity of the Spirit in the bond of peace."[13] Issues like the work of Christ on the cross and His resurrection should be agreed on and might be considered "closed-hand" issues. This is not to mean that you cannot invite others who may disagree with your "closed-hand" beliefs into your community. You should invite others. But, your core community, who has made these commitments to one another, should be in agreement. And, if others decide to join you, at some point, those beliefs should be made clear. Ultimately unity is revealed in full agreement to be bound together as citizens of the same Kingdom under the Lordship of Christ.

Goodwill. Seeking goodwill is directed toward individuals outside of your Christian community. This includes not only other Christians, as your brothers and sisters in Christ, but also all people.[14] We are stewards of God's good grace. We get to experience the fullness and perfection of it by extending it to those outside our gathering. We should never be a burden to our community-at-large, but rather contributors to our society, in helpful and life-giving ways. We are to be light to the dark areas of our culture and salt to those areas that require it. We must seek to build and maintain a reputation that causes others to "recognize that [we] have been with Jesus."[15] The truth of Christian community is that even those not in the community benefit from God's goodness toward us.

GCC Communally and Willingly ***Submits*** to…

The Word. When we speak of submission in the biblical sense, we are not talking about forced subservience. Instead, biblical submission is the willingness to yield to another's will or authority, primarily Jesus'. The Apostle John identifies Jesus as The Word in the opening sentences of his gospel account.[16] In this context, Christian community carries forward that revelation by submission to Jesus as the spoken *Word* of God. Likewise, a community seeking to walk like Christ challenges one another to submit to the entire counsel of God found in the Bible.

One Another. Christians commonly refer to this type of submission as "accountability." Unfortunately, accountability is only as effective as you are willing to be honest with each other. Too often, shame, guilt, or pride, coupled with the lack of authentic Christian community, prevents honest accountability. For submission to contribute to our growth toward Christ-likeness, it has to occur through obedience to the New Command. In GCC, members are committed to challenge each other to be in individual submission to one another. This does not mean that you are submitted individually to every member of the community. However, it does mean, you commit yourself to be mutually submitted to a few specific people, preferably the same gender. Not everyone in the group will, or should, know all of your "stuff," but someone should. In a healthy community, mutual submission can be practiced between multiple members at once. For example, my commitment to purity should cause me to seek submission with someone who is finding, or has found, victory, in Christ, in his or her purity. Likewise, if that person struggles to manage their finances, I wouldn't necessarily submit myself to them in that area of my life. Instead, I might seek out a different person who has victory there.

Additionally, the Greek word for *submit,* in Ephesians 5:21, is *hupotasso* and means to make yourself subject to another, typically in service to them. It means to place one's self under the others in service to one another. If this is occurring mutually, then there is a continual cycle of assessing and meeting each other's needs. This type of mutual submission involves all members trying to outdo one another in service to each other. It's essentially a race to the bottom, in which members willingly make themselves low and, in the process, raise up Christ. That's the New Command in action. Mutual submission is built out of intentionally investing in relationships both members give and yield to the authority, in Christ, of the others, in service to each other.

The Body. Submission to the Body has to do with yielding to the movement of the Holy Spirit within the community. It centers on collectively trusting that your fellow Saints are seeking God and His wisdom. It has to do with corporately taking issues and concerns to God and then trusting the collective wisdom of the Body as they submit to the counsel of the Holy Spirit. When we commit to submitting to those in the Body, it is out of a willingness to seek unity. We should also understand authority, both Christ's and that imbued by the Holy Spirit to our fellow Christians, "out of reverence for Christ."[17]

A commitment of challenge might be verbalized as:

We challenge each other to seek God, unity, and goodwill and to submit to the Word, one another, and the body so that we may walk as Jesus walked.

Acts 2 and the Commitment to Challenge

In addition to the numerous biblical references already noted, we can also see the early church challenging each other through seeking and submission in Acts 2:42-47. The passage opens by telling us each member *"devoted themselves to the apostles' teaching* and the fellowship." This passage reveals multiple truths. Not only were they committed to seeking God through the teaching of His Word, but also unity, as seen in their devotion to *fellowship*. Their willingness to be united in "one body and one Spirit"[18] prompted them to seek God and unity by "attending the temple" together and "breaking bread in each other's homes" daily.[19]

We also see a commitment to seek unity and submit to one another in verse 44. This verse shows us that all the believers were together and had all things in common. This is also a reference to their willingness to maintain one heart and mind in one Spirit. It seems clear that submission was a key ingredient to their community. Again, in verse 42 we can see that they submitted themselves to the apostles' teaching. This was not necessarily a reference to the believer's submission to the apostle's authority. However, there is an allusion it, but it more directly points to the Word of God being spoken into and over them.

To Spur Each Other On

Lastly, in verse 47 we can see their willingness to seek the goodwill of those around them. Many biblical commentators agree that "having favor with all the people" is easily interpreted to mean that the community of believers garnered the respect of all people, even unbelievers. This respect was gained through their devotion as followers of Christ and their unrestrained generosity and charity. While verse 45 does point to their care for those in the Body practicing the New Command, it likely extended beyond that. Verse 45 also suggests that the believer's generosity extended to all who had need, likely meaning all people in their immediate community, even unbelievers. This is obedience to the New Command, compelling them to obedience and fulfillment of the Second Command. This type of generosity and love would undoubtedly result in the goodwill of those around them.

Living in genuine community with other believers is a significant commitment that should spur each other on to love and good works. The ability to urge or encourage another person toward loving and serving others is no easy task. It is likely the most intense and difficult commitment that you'll make. But, even though it isn't easy, it's good. But more than good, it's how we experience Jesus. Community with other believers exposes us to the reciprocal love that Jesus desires all of His followers to know. And that starts with knowing that God loves you so that you can accept the love of your brothers and sisters so that you can practice the New Command; it's knowing and practicing. And our practice is a commitment in action. It is the commitment to remain connected to other believers through gathering together and also to challenge one another to walk as Christ through mutual seeking and submission. When we do that, we are truly answering the call to go make disciples of all nations.

Three Commands

8

TO GO AND MAKE DISCIPLES

Go, therefore, and make disciples of all nations, baptizing them in the name of the Father and of the Son and of the Holy Spirit...
~ Matthew 28: 19 ~

BECAUSE LOVING YOUR NEIGHBOR primarily involves expending love and loving each other is intended to be a replenishing love, I hope that we, as Christians, would first focus on building a healthy community of New Command practicing people. In doing so, we would fully experience what it means to love God and move toward loving our neighbor, which involves being His witness. But what does it look like to be transformed into the likeness of Christ?

Jesus was clear about why He came. He did not come to condemn the world, but rather to save us.[1] He even told Zacchaeus, you know the wee little man, He came to seek and save the lost.[2] If we're going to be His followers, we need to focus on the same mission. We've discussed at length that Jesus' New Command is the crux of the New Covenant, which allows us to experience the fulfillment of the Old Covenant. But, none of that matters if we try to do that disconnected from the reason that Jesus came. Loving each other should always flow toward loving our neighbor, and loving our neighbor should always be about an invitation into the Kingdom. An invitation into His kingdom should always create disciples. That is missional community; love = invitation = disciples.

And while that is typically the traditional flow, and certainly works, discipleship is about teaching others to obey His commands, the New Command. I assume that you have already confessed belief in Jesus and, if you attend church, should be surrounded by people who also believe. If that's

To Go and Make Disciples

an accurate assumption, it's time to begin discipling each other. That means committing to more than a weekly bible study. When you've practiced that long enough, the Holy Spirit will lead you, both individually and communally, toward being His witness to unbelievers.

Many people often include the Great Commission[3] in the list of Jesus' commands. That's fine, except that it wasn't really a command. The only place it says "commission" is in the sub-headings added by bible-translators. The word "commission" does mean "command" or "directive," but Jesus didn't say it was a command; remember, He was intentional when He used the word. "Commission" can also mean, "assign a task" or "give authority," and He certainly did that before telling them to go make disciples.[4] But that still doesn't make it a command. Remember earlier when I asked us to consider a different view of the Great Commission? If we look at it in the context of how Jesus gained His disciples, it was always by invitation. And that's what the Great Commission was, a Great Invitation. Jesus invites His disciples to invite and teach others in the same way He did them. He was, in essence, saying, "Join me in this grand mission of inviting and teaching others to love and forgive, to know the Father and Me, and to see Heaven brought to earth." Jesus' "go" was the same invitation He gave His disciples when He said, "come." He was saying, "Come, and I will show you how to live an abundant life, a real and true life, that you may show others how to live by revealing Me, who is Life."

So many churches get hung up on creating programs to ensure that discipleship is occurring. I've been part of so many of those meetings. The intention behind it was always good. We wanted to make sure that people in the church were gathering and growing beyond their Sunday morning Christianity. Usually, discipleship programs took the form of weekly small-groups, which were just smaller versions of Sunday morning. I don't want it to sound like I think that weekly small-groups are bad.

On the contrary, I love my weekly group, but the difference in weekly small-groups and genuine discipleship is what occurs outside of that second weekly meeting. The real question becomes, is your weekly small-group just another Christian event that you can afford to miss with no consequence? Or, is it a launching point for growing more deeply in relationship with other Christians, while you become more like Jesus? Regardless, we seem to, as we usually do, complicate something Jesus made pretty simple.

It appears that we have dismissed the way that Jesus, and later the Apostles, actually disciple people. We've tried to distill the practice of living a life committed to learning with and from others, into one or two 90-minute weekly sessions. Discipleship requires the opportunity to imitate, and that only comes by being involved in real life with other followers of Jesus. Gathering to eat, movie nights, and kid's soccer games bring great opportunities to showcase Christ-likeness to each other, beyond getting together to discuss the sermon notes. If you don't think so, then I encourage you to go to any kids sporting event and watch for the parent that explodes on the referee. Then, in front of your fellow believers, deal gently and sincerely with that parent. That's a legitimate discipleship moment. Real-life moments are the best place to display Christ-likeness. That's how Jesus discipled the first twelve.

When I said that we complicate something that Jesus made simple, I'm not saying discipleship is easy. It isn't. Living your life intentionally focused on allowing others to imitate you, especially when you know that you will get things wrong, is a difficult way to live. It's like going to any party and passing on a piece of cake level hard. But the idea is simple. And, Jesus didn't just leave us hanging to try and figure out how to do it on our own. He sent the Holy Spirit to enable us. He provided gifts to the Church for equipping the Saints to do the work of the ministry, i.e., witnessing and making disciples (Ephesians 4: 11-12).

EQUIPPING SAINTS

Writing to the Ephesians about unity and growing in Christ, Paul reminds them that it is the same spirit who brings unity that also gives some of us as gifts for equipping all of the saints. And why is He equipping us? We're equipped for the work of the ministry, meaning the administering of the gospel and the meeting of other's needs, to build the body of Christ. Literally, this means to promote and educate each other for growth in Christ; discipleship, so that we might expand His Kingdom. And we are to do this work until we are unified in our faith and knowing Jesus, so that we may become mature, reflecting Christ as we grow. Simple, right?

The big deal here is that we've again confused and complicated these gifts to the church. We've taken His gift, which is for the benefit of the receiver and conflated it to a position of superiority. Sadly, most congregations exist for the pastor, instead of the pastor for the people. Before we dive into what discipleship consists of, I want to make sure that we understand the five equippers of the Saints. These gifts to the church were given "for the training of the saints in the work of ministry."[5] This means that their primary ministry, or at least the one they're best equipped to perform, is discipling and teaching the Saints. The equippers are preparing the Saints to take the Good News into the world to glorify Christ. Those five equippers are apostle, prophet, evangelist, shepherd, and teacher.

Apostle

There is some debate as to whether this gift still exists in the church today. Of course, I know some churches use the word as a title, but that doesn't mean that they're necessarily an apostle in the original sense. Apostle, in general Greek terms, refers to a person sent on a specific mission with the full authority of the sender. In that context, we are all commissioned as ministers of reconciliation[6] and might be considered apostles if that were the only criteria. However, while the responsibilities of the apostles included preaching and teaching, it also included an administrative aspect. This took the form of establishing and structuring new churches, which included the commissioning of new teachers and pastors. Apostles were akin to missionaries, focused on the expansion of Christ's kingdom, but not all missionaries were apostles. Whether or not they are still an active gift to the church, apostles were/are typically itinerant, responsible for establishing The Church, and to some degree were responsible for caring for the welfare and life of the Christian community.[7]

Prophet

This is another gift to the church that some debate as to whether it is still in use today. When Jesus was commissioning the Apostles, there were a few who operated as Prophets, similar to the Old Testament. These New Testament prophets spoke, with authority, the words of the risen Jesus. They were likely most active during worship settings, as a means of encouraging and building up the body of believers through revelation. They might have acted as roaming preachers, traveling between churches, and preaching spontaneous messages, but there is plenty of indication they were most active as members of specific bodies. They were also gifted with identifying particular people and tasks assigned by the Holy Spirit and even equipped the saints with spiritual gifts.[8] In today's setting, this gift to the body for building up the body in similar ways. This does not include new direct revelation from Christ but is instead a reiteration of biblical truths as they apply directly to the teaching and building of the body. This may also include prophetic words for specific individuals and equipping and confirming in the saints the spiritual gifts necessary for their assigned task.

Evangelist

Evangelists are for declaring the Good News of Jesus. They are proclaimers and preachers of God's word but can deliver it in a simple, yet powerful and trustworthy way. They are the ones that hear God beckoning to the lost to come home and boldly extend the invitation. One of my best friends is gifted this way. I tell him often that I need him in my life to train me up in evangelism to better prepare me to share when the Holy Spirit prompts.

Shepherd

The other name for this gift is "pastor." Shepherds are those responsible for the direct care of the flock. They're gifted for attending to the hearts and needs of the flock to draw them closer to Christ. Pastors are people persons. This can be confusing, as the title pastor is used by most churches to designate their leader, who admittedly does not always fit the people person mold. In fact, they try to interchange the idea of pastoring with that of teaching, then hiring other "pastors" to care for the people. That isn't to say that teachers don't shepherd people. D. Marion Clark addresses this in his article, "The Servants." He says, "[The shepherd teacher] sees teaching as the means by which he nourishes the hungry soul and binds up the wounds of the broken soul. He is rewarded, not so much by how well his people are able to recall the information he gives, but rather by how strong their faith is growing and by the transformation taking place in their lives."[9]

Teacher

There is some debate about whether shepherd and teacher are separate gifts. This question is based on the grammatical structure of Ephesians 4:11. In every translation, there seems to be a clear separation between the first three gifts and none between the last two. What is clear is that all of the four previous giftings include the necessity of being able to teach. Regardless of whether or not it is a separate gift, teachers did hold a specific function apart from the others. While a prophet was charged and gifted with the preaching of God's word, "the teacher explained what the prophet proclaimed, reduced it to statements of doctrine (read truth and belief), and applied it to situations in which the church lived and witnessed."[10] Likely shepherds and teachers are the same office. Still, it only matters insofar as a pastor understanding that he or she is responsible for teaching and explaining, those in their keep, the truths of scripture, so they are equipped to do the work of the ministry.

These gifts to the church quite literally exist for discipling those in the body. I would almost say that while they should be actively using those gifts to invite unbelievers into the Kingdom, as gifts to the Church, they should be primarily focused on equipping the Saints to do that work. We can see the Apostles make a move toward that distinction in Acts 6 when they appoint people within the body to do the work of the handling of food and the financial aspect of the ministry so they could dedicate themselves "to prayer and to the preaching ministry."[11] As we settle into our callings, to do the work and then equip others to do it, we again can look to Jesus to see what it looks like to make disciples, or help them to "grow in the grace and knowledge of our Lord and Savior Jesus Christ."[12]

JESUS' "HOW TO" FOR DISCIPLE MAKING

When Jesus gave His disciples, and us, the authority and invitation to "go and make disciples," He was precise as to what that meant. In his commentary, Matthew Henry points out that the commission was not "go to the nations, and announce the judgments of God against them, as Jonah against Ninevah, and as other Old Testament prophets." Instead, they and we are to go into all nations and admit people into His kingdom. We're to go to people and offer them the same invitation that Christ has offered us, to come and follow Him. Then we are to disciple or teach them to be like Him.

When Jesus gave that invitation and authority to go and do what He had done, He provided three elements for making disciples. In Matthew 28:19-20, He said, "Go therefore and make disciples of all nations, baptizing them in the name of the Father and of the Son and of the Holy Spirit, teaching them to observe all that I have commanded you. And behold, I am with you always, to the end of the age." (ESV) In telling us to make disciples, He says to baptize, teach, and behold.

Baptizing

I made the decision to be baptized when I was 14 years old. At the time, I didn't fully understand the purpose. Mostly I was confused as to whether or not it was necessary for salvation, but again I chose to be baptized and just didn't ask. Not to worry, I eventually came to understand the purpose of baptism.

Three Commands

The intent here is not to argue over doctrinal beliefs about baptism, but instead to point out the importance of baptism as a part of discipleship. I'm aware of passages like 1 Peter 3:21, which say, "baptism, which corresponds to this, now saves you (not the removal of the filth of your flesh, but the pledge of a good conscience toward God) through the resurrection of Jesus Christ."

Easily that passage can be used to argue baptism as a necessary element of salvation, but it isn't necessarily saying that. David Mathis, Pastor of *Cities Church* in Minneapolis/St. Paul and executive editor for *DesiringGod.org* (John Piper's website) does an outstanding job explaining this passage. He says:

> Baptism demonstrates objectively and externally the subjective and internal "Appeal to God for a good conscience." Baptism saves not as an outward act, but through the inward faith it expresses. Peter's statement hangs together on baptism expressing a saving and spiritually new condition of heart in the believer.

First and foremost, baptism is our first opportunity for obedience to Jesus. It is the first thing He says to do when becoming a believer, and it is our first act of identifying with Him. Mathis is saying that baptism is the physical expression of our confession of Christ. Throughout the New Testament, we see baptism accompany, almost immediately, a person's confession of Jesus as Savior.[13] It was an important part of the act of repentance, which is a turning from something and turning toward something else. We see this before Jesus calls for us to baptize disciples. In the same article, Mathis points to Mark 1:5 as an important reminder that people were coming to John the Baptizer to receive baptism as they confessed their sin. Again, this wasn't an act that removed their sin, but an external expression of their internal faith that God would forgive them. When Jesus shows up to receive baptism, He doesn't denounce it but instead participates in it.

What is clear is that for Jesus, baptism has significance regarding our entry into the Kingdom as confessed citizens; and that we enter into the kingdom under the confessed Headship of God the Father, God the Son, and God the Holy Spirit. When we participate in baptism, we acknowledge and accept the One who welcomes us into His Kingdom, imparts His authority and commissions us for the work of the kingdom.

As I've already alluded, baptism is also about identity. This act is symbolic of our connection and submission to Jesus, connecting us to his death, burial, and resurrection. It's our wedding ceremony. It's our public confession of our connection to Him. You can privately confess Jesus as your Savior, but baptism requires at least one witness to be present. We are saying, "I am with Christ." We publicly identify unity with Jesus. Baptism is what sets the foundation of our confession and reveals our connection to our Lord. Baptism is also the mechanism by which we can draw a line between our old, dead self, and our new creation. It is the visible point at which your resurrection begins. It is you declaring, "I am in Christ and I am new!"

We need to remember that Jesus included baptism in His commission to go and make disciples. That means baptism isn't your pastor's job, but rather the disciple-makers job, which is you. It should be your joy to baptize a new believer. Baptism is part of our participation in inviting and welcoming another citizen into the Kingdom. When Jesus spoke of His authority to commission disciple-makers, He included baptism under that authority. "Go and make disciples; baptizing them…" This is your commission and part of making disciples. Now, go and baptize.

Teaching

I realize that some are gifted as teachers to the body. I've sat under some great teachers. I've also seen and heard people teach who made me wonder who encouraged them to do so early in life. Those teachings were like watching some kid auditioning for *American Idol*, whose mom spent his whole life telling him how great a singer he was when in reality, his singing should have never left the shower. Unfortunately, instead of becoming an American Idol, he ends up becoming a viral video or meme. I realize that not all people are called to be teachers in a large formal setting. We can't all be Paul, you know?

But, if you're one of the so many Christians who I've heard say they aren't a teacher, you're wrong. You may not be some mega-church, conference-speaking pastor, but if you profess to follow Jesus, you're a teacher. Jesus told us to teach others as a part of making disciples. Jesus says explicitly, "…teach [disciples] to observe everything I have commanded you."[14] There you have it; you're a teacher.

At this point, you should be clear on what it is that Jesus commanded us to do, especially His New Command. And one of the first things we are supposed to teach new believers is what it means to obey, in a practical sense, the command to love each other. When Jesus tells us to teach others, He is telling us to instruct them how to carefully attend to everything He's commanded. We could get into the weeds of what He commanded; we could have done that at any point. But, the thing He made clear as the indicating factor of our connection to Him is His New Command.

When a rabbi took on a disciple, the disciple first learned by merely following the rabbi, or teacher, around. The disciple would stay within a few feet of the rabbi and mimic his actions. The disciple was not only trying to learn what the Rabbi knew but was also intent on becoming like him. Eventually, the disciple grew to look and act like the rabbi and would sometimes leave to teach others how to live that same lifestyle. In doing so, the disciple made it known that he had learned from that specific rabbi, allowing others to identify him with his teacher. And it wasn't just about imitation. The rabbi's lifestyle became so ingrained in the disciple that he was no longer imitating the rabbi. Instead, the disciple eventually became a literal reflection of him who he followed. It is the same with teaching people to live and love like Jesus.

When I hear another Christian say they aren't a teacher, what I hear is, "I don't know if I can show others what loving as Christ looks like." Jesus wasn't calling us to teach theology or exigent scripture, although you should be able to articulate the bible clearly. If you can't, then get yourself under a shepherd-teacher and learn how. Jesus was calling us to show people how to hold close the things He did in His time on earth. When faced with a woman in sin, He showed loving-kindness, with a leper, loving-kindness; with a cheating tax collector, loving-kindness; with people disgracing the temple, okay He flips tables; but then when faced with Peter's denial, He showed loving kindness. Jesus is calling us to take His commands seriously and to show others how to obey and guard them. The one that enables all the others is the command to love each other. Now, go and teach.

Beholding

The last thing that Jesus said in verse 20 was, "...and behold, I am with you always, to the end of the age." Jesus was encouraging the disciples; again, us included, to observe that He is still with us. In the Jewish culture, the rabbi/disciple relationship would typically end with the disciple leaving to teach other disciples and was not likely to see their rabbi again. Jesus is suggesting a different take here. He is asking us, as His disciples, to continue to see Him as present in our lives, as we teach new disciples. This is important because making disciples isn't easy. Keeping Jesus in view gives us the comfort and courage to live and teach what He has commanded. Beholding Jesus is how we remain in Him and He in us.[15]

A lot of translations use the word "behold," but the Holman Christian Standard Bible uses the word "remember." I like what the word "remember" suggests when considering Jesus being with us. When we behold, we may be tempted to merely stand and see. Granted, there is an awe in beholding Jesus that we can't avoid, but beholding may not always elicit action. Remembering, on the other hand, requires some intentionality. Remembering requires us to access the part of our brain that holds memory and assigns meaning. In doing so, we keep Jesus, and our connection to Him, tied to what we are doing and why we do it.

Remembering also calls us back to the other time Jesus calls us to remember, communion. One of the best ways to remember, according to Jesus, is the act of sitting, breaking bread, and drinking wine together. This is not an individual or solitary event as some churches have made it. Gathering in a big room with 350 people and receiving a wafer and a thimble of juice, only to sit quietly and take it when your heart is "right with Jesus" is not the intention of communion, let alone resembles anything close to the Lord's "supper." Jesus gave us communion as a *communal* event, centering on remembering His goodness and work on the cross, together.

I've seen churches do this well in a large-gathering setting. At one church I attended in Boise, the members took the elements and then gathered in a big circle around the main room of the church. There were close to 120 people in the service, but that didn't faze them from trying to take communion as a communal act of remembering. Once formed in a circle, facing each other, the pastor reminded everyone why we take communion, the goodness of Jesus, and that He will return. He also talked about how they were family, and the reason they were gathering was to remember Jesus because it is a crucial part of our walk with Him. And then they participated in communion together. It was beautiful. And it was the closest to what Jesus intended that I've seen performed in a group that large.

Regardless of how large or small the gathering, gathering to remember that He is with us is an integral part of disciple-making. Remembering helps renew our mind and drives forward our transformation into Christ-likeness. Remembering is what keeps us focused on Jesus. Remembering together is how we encourage each other in Him. Hebrews 10:19-39 talks about this type of assurance and encouragement. In verses 23 to 25, we see the writer draw our attention to the importance of maintaining our hold on God's promises and showing our concern for each other, so we can encourage one another toward loving others and doing good works. We do this by gathering and encouraging each other to remember God's promises and that Jesus is with us. Now, go and remember.

CO-DISCIPLESHIP

I remember the first time I had to respond to a call, as a police officer, by myself. I was young, probably 20-years-old. I had only been a street patrolman for a couple of weeks. It was late, close to 2 AM, and we had a routine report of a loud noise complaint. I say routine because it wasn't unusual to receive loud noise complaints on a Friday or Saturday night. The call was to an older area of housing. These houses were assigned to the younger and lower-ranking airmen on the base. I was nervous and a little on edge as I responded. I was the same age as many of those airmen who lived in that area. My nervousness revolved around the potential of there being alcohol involved, and the younger airmen weren't usually as level headed as the higher-ranking members. Most of the time, these were relatively easy calls. You would show up, check some identification, and ask them to quiet down. Usually, they complied, and you'd be on your way. But my apprehension during this call was that, especially if there was underage drinking, someone might decide to challenge my authority as a cop, even more so because I was near the same age, and they might fancy they could "take me." And it didn't help that I was potentially looking at dealing with a group of intoxicated people, by myself. That was always a gamble.

On this particular call, everything went well. There were around eight people in the house, and yes, they were drinking and playing cards, but their music was too loud. Everyone was old enough to drink, and they responded pretty respectfully. I asked them to turn the music down, they complied, and that was that.

Contrast that feeling with another time that I responded, with a partner, to a fight at the on-base nightclub. Because I was with a partner, I felt completely different. Even though I was responding to a situation where I knew that the people involved were drunk and aggressive, because I had a partner, I felt more confident and assured of my authority and ability to handle it. Of course, there was some worry; there always is when there's limited information as you go into a potentially dangerous situation. But, it was reassuring to know that there was at least one other person who was there for the same reason I was. I knew, showing up to that nightclub, that I had the support of another person with the same mission. That knowledge helped to reinforce my function. It's the same when we consider discipleship. We're all called to discipleship, but never as a solitary endeavor.

Co-Journers

In Luke 10, we see Jesus implement this principle. In this passage of scripture, Jesus sends out 70 disciples, all in pairs. That's 35-pairs of disciples who Jesus "sent ahead of Him in every town and place where He himself was about to go."[16] When He sent them, He warned them about wolves and encouraged them to find people of peace, instructing them on how to address both being welcomed and being rejected. When they returned, He had not lost one[17] and they were full of joy. Then Jesus revealed the Father to them. The Bible doesn't tell us why Jesus sent them out in twos, but there's plenty of scripture that can give us hints.

One clear reason is our call to unity. Passages like 1 Corinthians 1:10, Ephesians 4:11-13, Colossians 3:13-14, John 17:23, and Psalm 133:1, all speak of the goodness and importance of unity among God's people. Logically, if we are to spur one another on to love and good works, our unified nature requires us to journey together with others. In every situation, the presence of another Christian should bring about the presence and strength of Christ, for when two or three are gathered, there He is with them.[18] Sadly, I have been in gatherings where this does not seem to be the case. That's not to say that Jesus' promise to be present isn't real, just that the focus of one or both of the Christians was not on His presence and strength. It is crucial to our growth and transformation as disciples that we understand the weight of being with other Christians. If being a disciple about learning, then every interaction with another Christian is an opportunity to learn from Christ.

It also creates a better environment for being a witness to and serving our neighbors. That's not to say that you can't or shouldn't go out and talk about Jesus to others by yourself; on the contrary, we should, and I know it happens. But, there's a reason why missionaries from The Church of Jesus Christ of Latter-day Saints and the Jehovah's Witnesses go out in pairs. They are imitating what Jesus did with His disciples, and they know that there's strength in numbers. And regardless of their view of Jesus and His divinity, by going out in twos at the least, they take Jesus seriously when he said He was with them. Maybe, as His followers, we should also take this aspect of how Jesus established the flow of journeying together seriously.

Three Commands

Co-journeying is also where we can begin to make a distinction between being a witness for Christ and being a disciple-maker. The purpose of a witness is that of a sower. As a witness, you're planting seeds. You're introducing others to truth and love in hopes that the Holy Spirit leads them into all truth. Disciple makers are cultivators, focused on tending to growth and gathering the fruit of those seeds into the Kingdom. Remember, we baptize disciples into the Kingdom. Discipleship has to do with teaching new followers how to obey all the things He commands. So witnessing is focused on an invitation, and discipleship is focused on teaching those who have accepted that invitation. Surely there is a blending of intention here, and you would have difficulty separating the two, but there is a distinct point at which you transition from witness to disciple-maker; from sower/waterer to tender/harvester. And that is when we become co-journers, traveling with each other, and Christ, toward Kingdom living.

Life-on-Life

Probably one of the best examples of this co-journer mentality, outside of Jeff Vanderstelt's *Soma Communities*, is Francis Chan's, *We Are Church* movement. If you're unfamiliar with Chan, Google him later, but for now, I'll give you a brief rundown. He was the lead pastor of a church he planted, *Cornerstone Church* in Simi Valley, California, and once heard him say that they were one of the wealthiest churches in America. That matters because it helps put into perspective what Chan may have been wrestling with in the area of the Church engaging in serving each other.

Chan is also the author of several books. Arguably his most popular has been *Crazy Love* and *Letters to the Church*, both great. In 2012, he quit as the lead pastor of his church and moved his family to Asia to do missionary work. After a few years, they moved back to America and settled in San Francisco to be near his brother. From what I've heard him share, he had no real intention of planting another church and just had a desire to be with people. He wondered what the church could be if Christians just tried to do what the Bible said. So he and his family did.

In one story I heard him tell, he was walking down the street, praying, and a guy recognized him and stopped him to say hello. Chan shared that the guy was a little intimidating; recently released from prison, tattoos, and a previous gang member, that kind of thing. The man shared about how *Crazy Love* changed his life and that all he wanted was to be a good husband and father, as he followed Jesus. Eventually, the Holy Spirit prompted Chan to invite this guy and his family to live with him. Chan and his wife let them move into the master bedroom, and they began living as a family. Chan intended to model Christ in the context of real life. He was putting into action Paul's call to "imitate me as I imitate Christ."[19] The benefit was that it allowed the other family to witness all of what it means to follow Jesus amid living life. Chan figured that the best way to disciple them was to do it life-on-life. It was also the best way for each of their families to best experience Jesus and practice His New Command.

Of course, Chan makes it sound kind of easy; just move a family of new Christians into your home for six months, then poof, mature Christians. Obviously we all can't, and maybe shouldn't, make that the primary standard for how we disciple someone. But, it should spur us on to look at where we allow people into our lives. We should occasionally take stock of how much margin we have in our lives and consider who we allow into that space. I know that some will say that their family is their first discipleship focus. And no doubt there is a lot of responsibility found in discipling our children and even co-discipling with our spouse. But, if there is no one else, no other Christian you are investing in, outside of your family, you have to ask if you're taking Jesus' commission to make disciples seriously.

I always find it interesting that we, as a society, can make time for so many activities, but lack in the area of gathering to help each other grow in Christ. We will dedicate ourselves to waking up at 5 AM, five days a week, to meet a friend at the gym, but we can't work in a consistent weekly cup of coffee to talk through life. Or we drive our kids to soccer, dance, karate, and every other sport, but we can't manage to show up to a weekly small group gathering consistently. It's not that any of those other things are bad; on the contrary, they can be excellent. But somehow, our spiritual growth has taken a backseat to every other area of life. We've come to believe that as long as we go to church on Sunday, we'll be fine. Except, statistically speaking, less than 20% of churchgoers are regular attenders,[20] which we define as attending at least two or more services per month. Even when we use Sunday as an excuse, it seems that we fall woefully short of a good reason.

Sunday attendance wasn't what Jesus meant when He said to make disciples. In fact, Jesus would have counted the idea of only seeing each other or meeting together just one day a week as ludicrous. Jesus modeled what it was supposed to look like for three years. He lived with the 12. Jesus allowed them to see all of his life. He hid nothing from them.[21] They saw His compassion, joy, anger, sadness, and even His transformation. And He saw theirs. The only way the disciples could see what it meant to live like Christ was to watch His life and imitate it. It was the same for Paul. He spent 2 to 3 years after his conversion, living with other Christians. He was learning what it meant to live like Jesus.

Paul was allowing the Holy Spirit through other, more mature, believers to work in his heart. Life-on-life is the "model" of discipleship that Jesus demonstrated, implemented, and directed in His New Command. Obedience to loving each other can only occur by being with each other. Living life with other Christians allows us to see the life of Jesus more clearly. Any aversion we have to it or excuse we use to get out of it only reveals our distrust in or indifference to Jesus and those in his body.

Let me reiterate that I know it's not easy. It requires you to step out of your area of comfort and be real with other people. It's hard enough letting your spouse see your garbage, and now you have to let others see it? If you want to participate in discipleship, then yes, people will see your stuff. But, what if they tell others or leave or judge me? Some might, but maybe it's part of the growth process. Jesus dealt with all of that; betrayal, denial, rejection, and abandonment, and that was just the day surrounding His crucifixion. All the things that we fear from our fellow man, Jesus experienced firsthand. In light of that, you have to ask yourself how much better are you than Jesus? How closely and tightly am I allowed to hold onto my privacy, my desires, my needs, and my life, regardless of Jesus saying that's the sure way for us to lose it?[22] He experienced it all for the sake of making disciples, but we don't need to? Maybe that's a point of reflection for some of us. And to be clear, you may not *have* to experience those things to disciple well. It probably makes you a better follower to experience having to trust God through some of those things, but they are not necessarily directly connected to disciple-making. Although, I should note that Paul reminds us "…we suffer with Him so that we may also be glorified with Him."[23] And Jesus did tell us that we will have troubles in this world, but then encourages us to take heart because He has overcome this world.

My first experience with life-on-life discipleship was the college ministry I led. During that time, I spent a lot, nearly every day of the week, with other people in my life. There were coffee dates, ultimate frisbee games, Bible studies, dinners, hangouts, and worship nights. I was 33-years-old at that time, and most of the people I hung out with were 18 to 25 years old, and many were new Christians. Even though they were considerably younger, I knew, and often told them, how much they were helping me grow in Christ.

There was never a coffee meeting that I walked away from that didn't make it a little clearer what being like Jesus should look like for me. Since having people in my home and life is the standard, I intentionally continue to make space for others in it. That still doesn't mean it's easy. Some aspects of life-on-life living are challenging.

Mutual Submission

Submission has become a four-letter word inside our church and most definitely within culture, and rightfully so to some degree. Leaders throughout the history of Christianity have used the idea of biblical submission to control, manipulate, and outright abuse people, primarily women, but men, too.

It truly is a disgusting thing when someone manipulates something that is grounded in the goodness of God for their benefit. Submission has been so twisted that it has created a generation of churchgoers who don't understand it and/or refuse to participate in it. You might say we have PTSD, Posttraumatic Submission Disorder. Regardless of your current understanding of it, submission is a biblical principle, which originates from God, and a mandate for Christian's interactions with each other. We briefly talked about submission in chapter 7, so hopefully, we did establish some understanding, but it is crucial to understand it in the context of disciple-making. Within Christianity, healthy submission is when both involved parties willingly extending it to each other as an act of obedience to the New Command out of reverence to Jesus.

In Ephesians 5, Paul is instructing Christians on how they are to live with each other. In verse 21, he says, "submitting to one another out of reverence for Christ." This is a different type of submission than the one he uses in the very next verse (22) about wives submitting to their husbands. Verse 22 reads, "Wives, submit to your own husbands as to the Lord…"[24] Historically, men in the church have loved to quote this verse as a means of control and authority in establishing a hierarchical system in the church and their home. It's been the source material for perpetrating many cases of abuse in the name of encouraging women to be good biblical wives. Somehow, those interpreters missed the scripture right above it that calls for Christians to submit to each other.

This isn't a marriage book, but there needs to be a distinction made here between the two words. In speaking to wives, in verse 22, the Greek word for *submit* is *idios*. This word mostly has to do with the idea of "belonging to one's self rather than another person." It's about how a person acted concerning their personhood. It was primarily about with what or who the person willingly identified. Because it had to do with the person having the ability and choice to decide whom they aligned with, a slave could not practice or identify with *idios* type submission. This was because a slave would not have been considered his or her own person. In this context, Paul is speaking to a Greek community of believers in Ephesus, where the women would have more autonomy and social status than a Jewish woman. Paul is telling married women that a wife should "act as the wife of and identify with their husband." Paul is telling wives to live out who they are as the wife of their husband.

The word for *submit* in verse 21, which speaks to all Christians, is different. That word is *hupotasso* and means, "be subject to" or "arrange yourself under or subordinate to another." It means to be placed under, in service to, another person. Slaves during this time would have been *hupotasso* regarding their master, but it wouldn't have been willingly or by choice. God, through Paul, is calling all Christians to be *hupotasso* to Jesus and their brothers and sisters in Christ, and yes, that extends to marriage in a mutual sense. The difference between *hupotasso* of slave and a Christian would have been the willingness of their submission. A Christian would submit to other Christians out of reverence for Christ. A slave would have had no choice. *Hupotasso* is entered into willingly, as an act of obedience to the New Command. And it wasn't just for the church in Ephesus. It was the same idea that caused Paul to implore the Philippians to "Do nothing out of rivalry or conceit, but in humility consider others as more important than yourselves."[25]

While the idea of mutual submission may have been lost or intentionally tossed away, we're still called to submit to and serve other Christians willingly. I know it isn't easy and opens you to the possibility of betrayal and hurt, but maybe it's part of how we practice radical love and forgiveness. We're meant to be expert forgivers, forgiving in the same way that Father God has forgiven us.[26] Eventually we'll have to experience something that requires forgiveness. In my estimation, there's not a better place to practice this than a body of people commanded to practice an extreme style of love and grace? Again, I'm not saying that potential betrayal and humiliation are reasons to practice mutual submission, just that there are things that Jesus wants to draw out of us. Some of them require a *hupotasso* kind of living. To be clear, and move back toward Jesus, He submitted himself to God and man, and it took Him to death on the cross.[27]

Hupotasso submission is essential to discipleship. There's a difference between a newer Christian devoting him or herself to the teaching of a more spiritually mature Christian as a means of sitting under their knowledge and wisdom and choosing to serve each other mutually. There is no distinction in the level of maturity when it comes to serving. And it's about giving and receiving influence into each other's life. Practicing mutual submission is vital to influencing the lives of those you desire to see grow deeply in Christ. And, it is key to your own deeper growth in him.

LOVE IS THE GREATEST

I've mentioned a few times that I started writing this book over six years ago. What I haven't mentioned is that I didn't touch it for about two years during that time. It just sat on my computer, half done. Every so often, I would go to the file, open it, read some of it, and then just stare at the screen. I couldn't seem to finish it.

At first, I stepped away so I could think through it, but eventually, my discouragement kept me away as a few weeks became years. After a couple of years, I heard someone talk about mind maps, and I immediately knew it was part of my solution to help me to start writing again. Before starting, I changed two things. First, I built a mind map for each chapter. If you're not familiar with it, it's just idea bubbles that connect to and build off of each other. Second, I went back to handwriting, in pencil no less. All of a sudden, I could write again, and I was off and running with a renewed vision. I share that with you to tell you this next story.

About six months into working through my mind map and outline, I decided I needed to restructure the last three chapters if they were going to flow in a direction that made sense. I was working on redrawing the map for this chapter, and I had four idea circles, with the first three completed. I was sitting there staring at the last bubble trying to figure out how to end this chapter and lead into the next about witnessing to others. As I sat there, my four-year-old daughter climbed up next to me and asked what I was doing. I told her I was working on a map for my book. She asked me what that meant, so I explained it by saying it was for figuring out my thoughts and ideas. Then she pointed to the last circle and said, "Oh, you missed one." I said, "I know," and told her I was trying to figure out what was supposed to go there. Then she looked at me and said, "Hmm, maybe love."

Man. Out of the mouth of babes. It's moments like those that keep me convinced of a God who loves us and gives us what we need. At that moment, I felt God say, through my little girl, "It's a book about love. It's how I do everything. I AM Love. It's about my love, so end it with love." She's a smart kid. Maybe already, but for sure, in the future, she'll be smarter than me. I just hope she always sees God and love that clearly; that when something seems to be missing, it's probably love.

Love is Ministry, Ministry is Life

I once heard a pastor say that you never REALLY get to retire from ministry. I don't remember who said it, but I remember realizing the gravity of that truth the moment after hearing it. I had just given into God's call to enter vocational ministry and was still pretty oblivious to what that entailed; truth be told, I'm still not positive. After hearing it, I remember trying to figure out a way for it to not apply to me. After all, at the time that I heard it, I had been in the military for 15 years and was looking forward to retirement. Retirement after twenty years of service, while it may seem an antiquated system, is still one of the perks of serving in the military. I had this idea that I would retire at 38 years old, then pastor a church for 20 or 25 good years and spend my twilight years enjoying my family, writing, and occasionally speaking at some leadership conference or local church. To hear that I would never get to retire was kind of depressing. Many years have passed since then. If you let it be, time is an excellent teacher and bringer of clarity. Now, I have a different view of vocational ministry and even ministry as a whole.

Today I view ministry as a lifelong endeavor. I've become more of a "bi-vocational" ministry guy. I see and hear God calling all of us to make ministry a continuous part of our life because it is not something reserved for a select few. Ministry should be an ever-present part of our life. After all, ministry is about service. That's how Isaiah ministered to God; he served and gave to Him. He gave his worship, praise, and life to God. Because of our western cultural understanding of ministry, we assign the pastor the responsibility to "do" ministry because we pay him to do it. Maybe it's not a conscious decision or even an excuse, but it's how we seem to approach it and act toward it. Here's what I've come to learn; love is our ministry. And if we're all called to love, we're all called to ministry. In this way, ministry becomes our life, and we don't get to retire from life. If we're honest with ourselves, we're all called to ministry. We're all called to give and serve. We're called to give our time, our talents, our money, our hearts, and our love. We're all called to serve the hungry, thirsty, naked, oppressed, imprisoned, downcast, widowed, orphaned, and each other. We're called to give to and help believers, unbelievers, insiders, outsiders, the broken, the lovable, the unlovable, friends, enemies, and everyone else. That becomes the daunting and joyful realization that you never retire from ministry. The pastor who I heard that from wasn't talking about hanging up your "job" hat. He was talking about something far more significant and so much more impactful than a job. He was saying, in the area of giving yourself away for the sake of Jesus, you never get to retire; there is not an endpoint.

There's never a point in scripture when Jesus tells His disciples they can "hang it up." There never comes a time when those same Apostles assign those in the first century Church, or ours, a specific age in ministry when we can call it quits. The expectation for a disciple is a lifelong walk of receiving from God and giving it away to others. That's why Paul told the Philippian church that he pours himself out like a drink offering for their sake.[27] He was saying that he was being emptied as a sacrifice, joined with their sacrifice so that others might know Jesus. That's our call, and it's a hard one. And it becomes harder when ministry isn't about love, especially when you try to do it alone. That's one of the reasons that Paul never did it alone. He always had others with him, for comfort, encouragement, and strength, in Christ. And it was the same with Jesus. He chose to live His life with other people, practicing a giving, and serving love. It was the *only* way it could have been done. It's also how this hard calling becomes Jesus' light burden and easy yoke. It's how we get to rest[29] and not grow weary.[30] Making disciples is a life commitment, focused on following Jesus and obeying His command to love. When we do that, others will know we are His.

So Others Will Know

Jesus told the disciples to make disciples and be His witnesses, but only after He gave them the New Command. I think Jesus was intentional in the order He revealed these things; love, disciple, and witness. He was speaking to people who were His followers. Jesus was talking to people who had been with Him, who knew Him, and were learning to love Him and each other. They were living in community with Jesus and each other, learning what it meant to be like Him and live a life of love. The scene of Peter's denial makes it clear that everyone knew who the disciples were and that they were with Jesus.[31] It's essential to see the connection between being His disciple and learning to obey His New Command. The command to love each other was, and is, the distinguishing element that reveals us as Jesus' follower. In fact,

Three Commands

Jesus tells us directly that the purpose of us loving each other is to reveal Him to all people.[32]

I always used to chuckle at the quote, "Preach the gospel at all times. Use words if necessary." I'm not sure who said it. People attribute it to Saint Francis of Assisi, but there's no real evidence of that. It doesn't matter who said it; what matters is what it implies. The implication is that your life should reflect the gospel to people so much so that you shouldn't even need to use words. I chuckled because it's often more of an excuse not to have to talk about Jesus with others. Regardless, it's a cute sentiment, but my main problem with it is that the gospel is inherently verbal. It's a story. It's the story of God and man, separation, tragedy, love, redemption, reconciliation, and victory. Because of that, I can't get around the idea of not using words. However, in this specific passage, it seems like Jesus is putting some heavy emphasis on our actions being the vehicle for revealing Him and announcing our allegiance to Him. To that end, we should all engage in healthy self-reflection and evaluation of how well our community of people reveals Him. At the very least, our love for each other should be so resolute and otherworldly that it causes people to question its source.

The purpose and intention of the New Command is to enable us to live in and fully experience the goodness of the law fulfilled. It is the basis for how we disciple each other and *the* command that we are to teach others to obey. It should lead us into abundant life and help us become the fully realized and unified bride of Christ. In doing so, the product of our love for each other, the fruit of our obedience is the revelation of Jesus. When we love each other, people will know we are His. Our love for each other is unbreakably bound to our witness of Him, our discipleship of others, and how much we look like Him.

Image Bearers

A couple of years ago, my friend Adam, Lead Pastor of *Awaken Church* in Nampa, ID, preached a sermon that completely changed the way I understand the original sin that occurred in the Garden of Eden. He said that although an act of disobedience did occur, it was less about obedience to a rule and more about a rejection of God's truth and our identity. He pointed out that the primary thing the serpent causes Eve to question is whether or not we are like God. In Genesis 3, Eve explains that they are not allowed to eat from the tree in the middle of the garden because they "will surely die."[33] The serpent responds, "No! You will not die. In fact, God knows that when you eat it your eyes will be opened and you'll be like God..."³⁴ The serpent challenges God's truth by telling them they will not die and then challenges our identity by suggesting that we are not already will be like God, made in His image. The saddest part of Adam and Eve's original sin is that we were already like God. Genesis 1:27 says, "so God created man in His own image; He created Him in the image of God."

We had already borne the image of God, from the point of creation. We were, and are, like our God. Yes, disobedience occurred in the garden; Adam and Eve did something they were told not to do. The more significant issue, the one that humanity has struggled with since Adam and Eve, was the rejection of truth and identity. But there's a remedy for the whole thing. Jesus. He resolved everything. And even though His work is complete and whole, on an individual and personal level it requires our response. Our response to Jesus is our participation in the remedy. So the remedy for disobedience is obedience. And the remedy of rejection is acceptance.

When we obey the New Command, we are accepting our identity as the Bride of Jesus. As a church, we are His Eve, built out of His side. We recognize our identity as His, made in, and bearing His image. Our desire to love each other restores and rebuilds our identity and reveals who and whose we are, to all people. But to what end? Invitation. Everything in the kingdom is an invitation. Everything in the Kingdom is pleading, "Come back to God."³⁵ Loving each other reveals that we are made in His image so that people can join us in truth and identity.

So Others May Join

Throughout the entire Bible, we see God making attempts to set His people apart. He places Adam and Eve in the garden, sends Abraham to a new land, marks the doors of His people in Egypt, gives them the Promised Land, and even initially not allowing them to have a king. These are all attempts to set his people apart from all the other people in the world. And what about the law? Let's go back to that for a moment.

The law was also given as a means to set them apart from other nations and cultures around them. In part, it reveals God and distinguishes His people as different from other people. Seeing the Law fulfilled would have revealed people who were whole and wholly devoted to a perfectly loving God. That's why Jesus said He came to fulfill the law. In doing so, He was revealing a people who are whole and wholly devoted to the one true God. One of the ways that Jesus fulfilled the Law was by giving us the New

Three Commands

Command. The New Command calls us to a type of love that sets us apart from the world. It's what He was talking about in Matthew 20:26, when He said, "it must not be like that among you. On the contrary, whoever wants to become great among you must be your servant." The type of love He calls His people to is the type of love that causes you to put the other person above yourself. It's a love in service to the other. The New Command fulfills the setting apart of all God's people through extraordinarily loving each other in a way that reveals that we are His. This is inarguably "setting apart" language.

It is a setting apart that is purely invitation. If, throughout the Bible, God has sought to set His people apart, it also needs to be recognized that He intentionally invites outsiders into the fold. Again, we see this through His promise to Abraham "to bless all the people of the earth through him,"[36] the prostitute Rahab,[37] Ruth with Naomi and Boaz,[38] Jesus and the Samaritan woman, the Roman centurion, all of Paul's mission trips, and Peter's vision of the net and food.[39] God's message includes, and always has, an invitation into His Kingdom. When Jesus says, "that others will know we are His," He is keeping with the intent of invitation.

We love each other, in part, that we would be witnesses for His unifying love, so others would join us in the unity of following Him and teach them what it looks like to live in the Kingdom. This can only happen in an environment based on relationships, where love is freely exchanged between the members.

Relationships, Not Rules

I've written at length about the drastic difference between religion built on rules and community based on relationships. However, in the context of the connection between discipleship and relationships, there's more to consider.

One of the things I've always found difficult was talking with a new Christian about obedience to a set of commands. So many people label any command that they encounter with the moniker "rule." I think, as a church, a lot of us would rather avoid that conversation. You can see it in the way we talk and what we emphasize about following Jesus. Statements like, "It's about relationships, not rules" seem to be the way we get around telling people that they have to behave a certain way. And I get it; we're weary of the road that "commands" might lead down. We try hard to be careful of suggesting that Christianity is about behavior, lest we return to the 80s and 90s Behavior Modification Gospel era.

To Go and Make Disciples

Unfortunately, it's tough to get around the obedience thing, especially when Jesus says things like, "If you love Me, you will keep my commands."[40] In fact, His Apostles thought He was serious about obedience to His command, too. Every book of the New Testament, after Acts, is a letter from one of them that tells us how we, who are in Christ, ought to behave. The Apostle John even flat out says that if you say you love God but don't obey the command to love each other, you're a liar. That is a heavy thing to consider. Because of statements like that, we must give attention to what it means to be obedient and how it works in relationships with Jesus and others. How we understand obedience also plays into how we understand disciple-making; remember Jesus said we are to teach others to obey all He has commanded.

I think a good place to start is to clarify that obedience does not equal love, but love will always result in obedience. It's like this; think about your marriage or an intimate relationship if you're not married. How did you get there, to the point of actually loving that person? You followed the rules. They may have been unspoken, but you knew what they were, and you followed them. When you first met and started dating, you followed whatever rules allowed you to have another date. For example, because of your desire to know each other, you likely began to give up getting to know other people. At some point, you followed the rule of monogamy, which is the habit of having only one relationship at a time. You decided to date each other exclusively. You followed the rules because that is how you got to know each other and began building a relationship.

Eventually, you began to fall in love, not because of the rules, but because of the time, you invested in getting to know each other and developing your relationship. Your commitments to the "rules" created the boundaries and were the catalyst that allowed time to draw you closer together. When that happened, you began to "follow" the rules, not because you feared the consequences of breaking them, but because you loved the person and couldn't fathom betraying and hurting them. You do certain things and act in specific ways that now reveal your commitment and connection to the person, not the rules. It's the same with your relationship to Jesus and His bride. We might begin, as new Christians, learning how to obey His commands, which is often a commitment to learning and following the "rules." But then time and interaction draw you into a deeper connection. Eventually, you fall in love. And if it's in a community committed to obeying His New Command, it's easy to fall hard in love with Him. Then, when we fall in love with Jesus and His bride, we can't help but want others to experience it. Disciple-making is about building relationships. It is a natural outworking of experiencing Jesus' love to such a degree that we can't help but extend it to others.

In that light, discipleship becomes about relationships that make obedience a natural part of honoring Christ and His call to love each other. It turns out that the whole "Great Commission as an invitation" thing is about inviting people into a relationship where they get to learn to be loved and love others. When we view it that way, we want others to join us in knowing Him. It's also the way that we grow the Kingdom and see heaven come to earth.

Body Building

Throughout the years, I've had a lot of enthusiastic friends, some might say obsessed, with weightlifting. I tried it for a bit but then decided that the best way to avoid being injured was not doing it. I also wanted to be able to lift my arms above my waist, so that was a motivator as well. I also like pie more than the gym, so… One thing I learned from my brief engagement with lifting weights, and all my friends who still maintain that lifestyle, was that to grow the muscles in your body, you need proper nutrition. It required proteins, amino acids, and other supplements that I can't remember, to get the best results and build the body you want. It also requires a commitment to doing the work, adherence to the practices that are proven to create health, strength, and growth. And it helps to have a workout partner. It's a similar requirement when it comes to discipleship and building the body of Christ.

As I said, there are some great books on what it means to disciple and how to go about making disciples. Pastor and author, Mike Breen, has written several books on discipleship. One of them is titled *Building a Discipling Culture*. In it, he says, "Jesus has not called us to build His church. Our job, our only job, and the last instructions He gave us, was to *make disciples*." He goes on to explain that while his book offers some practical ways for making disciples, success in disciple-making is based on texture, or a feel, not just some structured program. He describes that texture as family. The feeling of family is what "fertilizes discipleship and helps us to grow."

Family is the fertilizer of discipleship. That means that the feeling of family is what nourishes growth in and of the Kingdom. The thing that distinguishes family as the texture versus another social structure is love. Jesus knew that. Again, that's why He gave us the New Command *before* commissioning us to make disciples. A healthy family is a family that practices loving well, and that goes for us as Kingdom citizens. A healthy body of Christ is one who practices loving well. That's because love covers a multitude of sins,[41] it's patient, kind, not selfish, bears all things, rejoices in truth, hopes in all things, endures all things, and never ends.[42] Love is what gives texture to family. And family is what gives texture to discipleship. Family nourishes and fertilizes discipleship so that it becomes about building the body into a kingdom of lovers: lovers of God, lovers of each other, and lovers of others.

Community is critical to this process. Without the support of your "work out" partner, you might become tired; you might quit. A Gospel-centered community of people, who are committed to loving each other well, are the ones who continue to provide the nourishment and fertilizer needed to keep going and keep growing.

Without learning to obey and live out the New Command, and then understand how it leads to and equips us for obedience to the Greatest and Second Commands, you can never fully know what it means to make disciples. Of course, you can flesh out the rules and then build programs and courses geared toward following them; we've been doing that for centuries. You can even create Bible studies and service project groups that give the appearance of obedience to the commands to love God and your neighbor. But in the end, all you're doing is building a program, and programs have a shelf life. But when we learn to obey the New Command, when we learn to love each other, only then do we become a family led by a good Father. And He's a Father who desires to have all of His beloved reconciled back to Him. And we do that through cultivating disciples who desire to make disciples.

CULTIVATING DISCIPLES WHO MAKE DISCIPLES

This brings us back to the idea of Gospel Centered Community. Remember when I said that a commitment to cultivating disciple-makers was the thing that moved us from GCC into a missional heart and mindset?

Within the context of a missional community, the idea of cultivating has a few applicable definitions. Cultivation can mean, "to develop or improve by education or training," "to promote the growth or development of," or "to devote oneself to developing or growing." When a community commits to cultivation, they are devoting themselves to developing and promoting the growth of disciples who make disciples. When we commit to this, we are answering Jesus' call to be His witness to the world.

Three Commands

When cultivating disciples who make disciples, we are creating a culture of going out. It is a culture in which we fully embrace our role as Ambassador,[43] which we will discuss more fully in the next chapter. Making disciples is an acknowledgment that the Kingdom is not exclusively ours, but rather is intended for all of creation. Cultivating disciples who make disciples moves us from the focus of growing in strength as a community toward increasing the size of the Kingdom. This is distinguished by the flow of love within GCC and GCMC. In GCC, we focus on giving and receiving love in a close and closed setting. It's about receiving the love of Christ poured out on His Bride. GCMC is about revealing the love of God to others. It's us pouring out the love of God on the lost. We do this through sacrifice.

Over the 20 years I served in the military, I participated in a lot of missions. The one thing that every mission had in common was sacrifice. While every mission required sacrifice, the most successful missions were ones that I willingly committed to that sacrifice. While it's true that work was completed during the missions where my sacrifice was forced, those missions never felt like a success in my estimation. When I believed in and was committed to the mission, my sacrifice came willingly.

And there was a lot of sacrifice involved in over 20 years of service. Sometimes that sacrifice required time. I missed a lot of holidays, birthdays, and anniversaries because of deployments, 20-hour workdays, and training exercises. Sometimes the sacrifice involved our resources. When the military moved my family and me to Japan, we went from a 2,200 square foot house to a 1,400 square foot four-plex. To meet the requirements of that mission, we had to sacrifice, or give up, our resources. And sometimes, the mission requires you as a sacrifice. I have a lot of military brothers and sisters who laid down their lives for the sake of their fellow member-in-arms and their country. For them, the sacrifice *was* self. The mission of Christ, to make disciples, is a commitment to willingly sacrifice for the sake of inviting others in.

GCMC willingly **Sacrifices**...

> ***Our Time.*** If your first thought, when I mention sacrificing your time for making disciples, is "I have no time," then you may need to reevaluate your priorities and adjust your schedule. Or, just admit that you're not ready to commit to Jesus' mission. Making disciples will require much of us, including our time. Jesus dedicated three years, of

nearly constant time, to developing His disciples. The Christians in Tarsus devoted almost three years to discipling the Apostle Paul before he went out. This should clue us in on the time investment required for making and growing disciples.

When we read about Christian communities throughout the New Testament, we see them dedicating huge portions of time to fellowship and growing together. They were always together, eating in their homes and attending Temple together daily.[44] Hebrews 10:24-25 is a verse that pastors popularly use to encourage people in Sunday church attendance. This interpretation reduces the importance that early Christians placed on gathering with one another as a matter of daily life. When the writer of Hebrews encouraged us to "not [stay] away from our worship meetings," the readers would have understood that as a reference to how they gathered in Acts 2. The new Christians recognized that the time they sacrificed to gather frequently was necessary to "stir up one another to love and good works."[45]

Our Resources. Few Christians would argue with the idea that God calls us to be generous with our resources. This isn't about "tithing." I don't care about how you interpret the tithe, although it does bear some importance on the communal gathering. Regardless, sacrificing your resources in the context of a community goes far beyond giving 10% of your income to a local church. Instead, it's about maintaining an open hand with all God blesses you with to meet needs and reduce burdens. In Acts 2 we read about the new Christians selling all they owned to make sure that no one had a need. In Matthew 19:21, we see Jesus tell a man to sell all he owns, give it to the poor, and follow Him. Jesus and the Apostles taught the complete rejection of materialism to emphasize a heart of extreme generosity. It wasn't about a Poverty or Prosperity Gospel, either. It was, and is, about a generosity within a body that identifies with Christ's sacrifice, as His disciples.

Our Self. There are many scriptural references that talk about sacrificing ourselves for the sake of Christ and our fellow Christian.[46] Jesus is clear that "whoever loses his life will preserve it."[47] And when it comes to sacrificing self, the primary element in this is love. Jesus, and later the

Three Commands

Apostles, continuously exhort Christians to love one another. Sacrifice of self will always spring out of love for Jesus and each other. It is a love built out of a desire to see others come to and follow Jesus well. When we sacrifice ourselves, we identify with Christ and His sacrifice. In doing so, we lay aside our desires and needs for the sake of those closest to us, so that Christ receives the glory. One of the best explanations for this type of love is in Philippians 2:3, which reads, "Do nothing from selfish ambition or conceit, but in humility count others more significant than yourselves."

A commitment of cultivation might be verbalized as:

We will cultivate disciples by sacrificing our time, resources, and self to make other connected disciples.

Acts 2 and the Commitment to Cultivation

When we read Acts 2:42-47, it is easy to see the heart of sacrifice present in the early church. One of the most explicit pieces of evidence is in verse 45. Shortly after Peter's Acts 2 sermon, many believed,[48] and they were together "selling their possessions and belongings and distributing the proceeds to all, as any had need." This verse makes clear they viewed their resources as a way to diminish the needs of those around them, both believers and unbelievers. This was them learning to love each other. This was the new Christian disciples being taught to obey Christ. This sacrifice and teaching also made them into disciple-makers. We see that in the investment of time they committed to gathering with each other. Three of the six verses[49] tell us that all the believers were together every day. This was a sacrifice.

They also gave themselves to the building up of each other in Christ and advancing the Gospel. How do we know that they did? Their commitment to making disciples is revealed in that "the Lord added to them those who were being saved."[50] All of their charity, generosity, and time they invested, and all of their willingness to give of themselves, for the sake of Christ, drew people to God. What is clear about the new Christians is that they were committed to cultivating disciples who cultivate other connected disciples.

Jesus did not call us to create converts. If all He required us to do is add people to the church, with no intention to lead them into becoming like Him, He would not have told us to teach them to obey Him. Frankly, we've tried that as a church, the seeker-friendly church would be an example of that, and it has just resulted in people who are Christian in name alone. It's also contributed to the large exodus of people from Christian churches in recent years. Our focus has to be both/and. Co-discipleship in a community committed to practicing the New Command is *the* way that we become like Christ and reveal Him to the world. Only when that becomes a reality are we equipped to interact with our neighbor in the way that Jesus instructed the religious expert when he asked who his neighbor was. Discipleship is where we learn to "go and do the same."[51]

9

TO GO AND DO THE SAME

"The one who showed mercy to him," he said. Then Jesus told him, "Go and do the same."
~ Luke 10:37 ~

WHEN JESUS TOLD THE STORY of the Good Samaritan, He was answering the Pharisees question about who we should identify as our neighbor, as noted in the Second Command, "Love your neighbor, as yourself." We've already talked at length about whom Jesus identified as our neighbor, so that's not the point of this chapter. However, it does set the foundation for what Jesus told the religious leader at the end of that story.

Jesus asked a question that forced the religious leader to answer his own question. We can speculate all day about why He did this, but Scripture is clear that they were trying to trap Jesus with His own words, so it's likely that Jesus, you know with Him being God, positioned his answer to make the expert answer. That way, the person with public authority was the one identifying the Samaritan as a Jew's neighbor. Remember, Jews didn't like the Samaritans, so for a Pharisee to acknowledge them as neighbors would've been a big deal. However, notice how the religious expert didn't answer using the word "Samaritan." Instead, he said, "the one who showed mercy." This was probably his way around saying something that would have landed him in trouble. Regardless, it looks like Jesus didn't need the religious expert to say the word "Samaritan" to make His point.

In his letter to the Galatian church, Paul echoes Jesus in telling them that loving your neighbor fulfills the entire law.[1] Both are saying that we love others and see the law fulfilled through mercy and compassion toward those around us. By obeying that command, we get to participate in and experience Jesus' fulfillment of the law.[2] And more than just participating in and experiencing it ourselves, it is how we introduce Him to a world that doesn't know Him; it's how we become witnesses and ambassadors for the One we claim to follow. I'm not trying to suggest this is easy. On the contrary, Jesus tells His disciples, and us, repeatedly that we will have tribulation.[3] You can read that as oppression, pressure, affliction, and distress because it means all of that. And almost more difficult to understand than the truth that we'll experience any of those things is that Jesus still sends us out into the world, knowingly, as sheep among wolves.[4]

SHEEP AMONG WOLVES

The idea that Jesus intentionally sends His followers out as sheep among wolves can be a hard pill to swallow. Surely a loving God wouldn't want us to get hurt, right? Well, it's not that simple. Being a witness is hard and often requires a lot of courage.

Over 20 years as a police officer has allowed me a lot of interaction with people who have been witnesses to some pretty bad things. Among those witnesses are those who are sometimes unwilling to share what they saw. But even as hard as it is to get someone to talk with a cop, especially today, nothing compares to the unwillingness to bear witness than my current job. I'm the Dean of Students in a public middle school in southwest Idaho, and I cannot tell you how often I hear, "Snitches get stitches." If you're not familiar with this term, it is pretty self-explanatory, but means, "If you tell, you get beat up." Since I deal mostly with discipline issues, like trying to pin down details of a fight or where the marijuana came from, I hear that statement a lot, and it wears on my nerves. Getting witnesses to share willingly isn't always easy.

As I look around the church landscape, I feel like a lot of us operate under the same principle when it comes to being a witness for Jesus. It's almost as if we're stuck on the idea that if we share, we are inviting tribulation and that being sheep among wolves means that they'll win. It appears that many of us are operating from the belief that "snitches get stitches" so we don't share Jesus. When we operate under that belief, we are allowing it to overshadow the truth of His strength and goodness, and that He sent the Holy Spirit to be our Advocate.[5]

It's important to acknowledge that being a witness for Jesus isn't wholly safe. The word *martyr* is the Greek word that means *witness*. We've come to associate being a *martyr* with being killed. To be fair, the fear of violence and persecution against Christians is well-grounded in history and is a valid fear.

Three Commands

And it isn't a fear that we reserve for antiquity; it happens today. We watched it happen throughout the 20th century with the building of the Soviet Union in the early 1900s and Mexico under Benito Juarez. Hitler persecuted Christians during World War II. Even today, we see Christian persecution in many Arab countries and countries throughout Africa, where Muslim extremists operate. And what about the many Chinese Christians who have to remain mostly underground to avoid persecution? Christian persecution isn't an unjustified fear. And while all of that is true, the comfort of free religion we experience in America has allowed us to dismiss that being a witness, a martyr, was the standard role and just a part of life in the 1st century Church.

Even still, it isn't like we didn't know it would happen. Jesus was clear about us being sent as sheep among wolves. And wolves eat sheep. Fortunately, He was also clear about His power and that He has overcome this world. Every time He spoke about the dangers associated with following Him, He always reminds us of His power and how He goes before us.[6] We knew at the outset or at least should have, that the world would not universally welcome the Message we carry.

Before Jesus gave us the New Command, before He told us the world would hate us, He talked a lot about remaining in Him. In John 15:1-8, Jesus implores us numerous times to remain in Him as He is in the Father. And John 15:5 he says, "I am the vine; you are the branches. The one who remains in Me and I and him produces much fruit." Jesus is using body language here. He's talking to people, not a person. He's telling the disciples, and us, that they are branches connected to Him, the Vine, and together they will bear much good fruit. Grapevines have many branches that all bear fruit together. A vine with a single branch may bear fruit, but certainly not enough to feed many. However, many branches bear much fruit. Jesus is laying the groundwork for how we'll love each other and how we'll overcome the very real persecution of a world that hates us.

They Hated Him First

Jesus directs us toward unity with each other, in Him, as the formula for loving each other and as the antidote for the world's hate. We find both acceptance and refuge when we are united together in Him. I often find it curious when I hear a Christian act surprised that a non-Christian doesn't act lovingly toward them. It's as if the Christian, with their new understanding of love, can't grasp why a non-Christian doesn't understand it the same way. What confuses me more is when Christians become withholding of or withdraw love when a non-Christian doesn't respond in kind. Love your neighbor is *our* mandate, not theirs. If we are to go into a hurting and lost world, we must expect that hurt people will end up hurting people. They may do it unintentionally, although some will be intentional about it, but hurt always begets hurt.

But we are called to love people, to comfort the hurting, and even pray for those that persecute us. If you are the recipient of Christ's amazing love, you have a responsibility, and it should be your joy, to give it away to others. You'll always have a hard time doing that if you don't realize and accept that you may get hurt in the process. It doesn't make it hurt less; it just helps you respond appropriately and reminds you where your help comes from.[7] My friend, Grant Clark, is probably one of the best at understanding this. He is, by far, one of the most loving people I know. He's experienced hurt, but understands this and depends on Jesus to walk him through it. He has a saying that goes, "Where there's people, there's poop." The idea is that caring for and loving people can and will get messy if you are engaged in their lives. You should expect the mess that comes with life. Our mess is the reason that we need Jesus. People need to know that. And how else will they know about the amazing love of Christ, unless someone tells them?

Unless Someone Tells Them

In his letter to the Romans, at the end of chapter 10, Paul is talking about Israel's rejection of God's message. He opens with a question, "How can they hear without a preacher?"[8] I find it odd that Jesus puts the responsibility of telling wolves about Him on to sheep. Then again, His is an upside-down serve-to-lead type of kingdom. He is the spotless lamb, sacrificed on the altar by the very wolves He came to save. It's the way the Kingdom works, least made full, last made first, and all that. It's clear that we are meant to go out, as sheep among wolves, and love the very ones who would hate us. It's why He told us to love our enemy. And why we offer our other cheek and carry their armor the extra mile. It is how we bring good news to a world drowning in the bad. It's also how we come back to trusting that *He* has overcome the world.

In all that sheep and wolves talk, He never told us to go and do it by ourselves. It's another reason why Jesus sent the disciples out in pairs in Luke 10:1. This is part of our bearing with one another in unity.[9] We are communal cross-bearers, carrying one another's crosses, bearing each other's burdens, as we follow Jesus through, sometimes hostile, streets. And so we go and preach, so they can hear about Him, believe in Him, and call on Him.[10] And in doing so, we become the neighbor in the Good Samaritan.

NEIGHBORING WELL

When Jesus told the story of the Good Samaritan, it certainly would have caused a stir. Remember earlier when I pointed out that the Pharisee wouldn't say "the Samaritan" acted as the neighbor, but instead mentioned the man's actions when Jesus asked? And what was the action he mentioned? He said, "The one who showed mercy to him." Jesus' response was simple. He said, "Go and do the same."

Jesus is serious about what it means to love our neighbors genuinely. Of all the various laws He could've mentioned as the most important, He chose loving God and loving our neighbor. And not only did He choose two commands as His answer to a question with which they were looking for a single command, but He also gave them equal weight. Then He said it was these two commands that encompass, or include and bring about, everything the Law and the prophets spoke of. In other words, everything God ever gave us, through Moses, David, Solomon, and any of the other Prophets, is summed up, points to, and is brought to fulfillment by loving God and our neighbor. If we are going to neighbor well, we are supposed to be the Samaritan in that story.

It's important to point out, in keeping with the "sheep among the wolves" theme, what Jesus is preparing the disciples, and us, to accomplish. He uses a Samaritan helping a Jew on purpose. It was the Jews who had amity toward their Samaritan neighbors. Samaritans were looked down on and treated poorly, even harshly, by the Jews. There is no way that a Jew would willingly accept help from a Samaritan. And a Samaritan knew enough not to offer it. So, Jesus goes ahead and makes the Samaritan the good neighbor, helping a person, who by all accounts, is his enemy. Not only that, He makes the defining action of the Samaritan treating the Jew as a neighbor, mercy.

Have Mercy

The answer Jesus was looking for from the Pharisee was that the neighbor was the one who showed mercy. It was so much about mercy Jesus instructs the Pharisee, and us, to "go and do the same." This prompt is huge. In identifying who our neighbors are, Jesus makes showing mercy a defining factor for what it means to love them. And this is not a new thing. We can go back to the prophet Micah, who prophesied 700 years before Jesus. It was

To Go and Do the Same

God, speaking through this prophet who told the Israelites the same thing. Micah 6:8 says, "He has told you, oh man, what is good; and what does the Lord require you to do but to do justice, to love kindness, and to walk humbly with your God?"[11] Other translations like the KJV, NIV, and NLT all use the word *mercy* instead of *kindness*. And what is kindness if not mercy and compassion toward another?

Mercy is a strange, often misrepresented, thing. The movies depict it as a king refraining from beheading his rival. We see criminals beg for it in court, and sometimes authority figures offer it, but it is often with reluctance and always from a position of superiority. The dictionary does define it, in part, as compassion or forbearance of punishment shown to an offender by someone in power. We have certainly embraced this definition and assigned it to how we relate to and view God's mercy.

It is true and biblical that all have sinned and fallen short of God's glorious standard[12] and that sin is offensive to God.[13] It is also true that God will judge people according to their sins and deeds.[14] But what if the primary mercy that God offers more closely resembles the Samaritan in the parable? What if God's mercy is not primarily an act of forbearing punishment against us as some vile offender? What if God's mercy is an act of compassionate treatment and caring for His people, who are in distress?

The word for mercy that the Pharisee responds with was *eleos*. The word is similar to a Hebrew word, *checed*, used in Hosea 6:6, which Jesus uses when He speaks in Matthew 9:13. He is quoting God, who, through Hosea, says, "For I desire mercy; and not sacrifices." Some translations use the word "loyalty" or "steadfast love," but the implication and meaning are the same. What Jesus and God, because He only says what the Father commands Him to say,[15] make clear is that He desires that we treat our neighbor with compassion, steadfast loving-kindness, and even loyalty. And not necessarily the same loyalty that unites us to our Christian brothers and sisters, but a loyalty that draws us to them as God's creation, divine just as we are. It's a type of loyalty that causes us to look at them with the same affection that God does. His desire is for their healing and wholeness, to be brought home, and joined to Him.

When we view God's mercy purely as an act of forbearance of punishment, we can easily displace or disregard His love nature. When we do that, we see others from a position of an offender and step into the place of God, offering the nonbeliever the opportunity to receive "mercy." We are operating from a place that suggests we received a reprieve from punishment by throwing ourselves on the mercy of God's court, so there's no way anyone else is coming to Him except in that way. We have the formula for it, and they will throw themselves at our feet, beg for mercy, and then we'll introduce them to the King. We would never say that, but we certainly act that way.

But that's not the kind of mercy about which Jesus is speaking. Showing mercy to our neighbor is intended to look more like the Samaritan in the parable. It should be compassionate, kind, and loving. It should be a vehicle for caring for them in their distress so that they can walk into a second life. When we view mercy that way, we start to see our neighbor as someone in need of God's care. Then we bind their wounds and carry them to the inn. When we get there, we give them to the one that can tend their wounds and heal them. The innkeeper, in this instance, is Jesus. We're bringing them into the security of Christ. Only then can we understand that the most significant distress a person will ever experience is separation from God the Father. We need to direct all of our work of loving our neighbor and being His witness toward caring for them in their distress so that we might undo it.

Doing No Wrong

Throughout my life, I've heard Christians say things like "love without truth isn't loving." The actual quote, as far as I can tell, is from, pastor and author, Warren Wiersbe, and goes, "truth without love is brutality, love without truth is hypocrisy." The quote is undoubtedly right. I've often heard it used as an excuse to present the truth of God to nonbelievers as an accusation and in very condemning ways. Even then, it's always packaged in something meant to look kind of like love. The implication here is that giving biblical truth, to expose their offense toward God, is the most loving thing you can do. But it mostly comes across as accusatory and self-righteous, and really kind of jerky.

When we look at the Good Samaritan parable, we see a different kind of love. We see a love that God, through Christ, is continually offering. It's a love that builds up and draws close. It tends to wounds and ends distress. It's a love that does no wrong. That is the kind of love God requires, not just desires when He tells us to love our neighbor. As I've already mentioned, loving your neighbor is connected explicitly to how Jesus fulfills the law and how we participate in its fulfillment. Romans 13:8-10 is pretty explicit on this point. It reads:

Let no debt remain outstanding, except the continuing debt to love one another, for whoever loves others has fulfilled the law. The commandments, "You shall not commit adultery," "You shall not murder," "You shall not steal," "You shall not covet," and whatever other commands there may be, are summed up in this one command: "Love your neighbor as yourself." Love does no harm to a neighbor. Therefore love is the fulfillment of the law.

In this passage, the Apostle Paul is telling us that we owe others love. He comes right out and says we owe the debt to love one another and that it is what fulfills God's law. Then he lists four of the original Ten Commandments and adds, "whatever other commandments" just to make sure there isn't any confusion that he is, in fact, including all of the Law. He ends by telling us that all of them are summed up in the command to "love your neighbor as yourself." He is saying what Jesus said in Matthew 22:39-40. Paul then expands on that concept and tells us that not only does it fulfill the law, but that it does so by doing no wrong to a neighbor. I know we would never consider sharing Biblical truth as "doing wrong," but think about the implications of what Paul is talking about here.

In the context that Paul uses it, the word *wrong* actually means "of bad nature" and "injurious or destructive" toward another person. It addresses a deeper level of thinking or view that we may have toward our neighbor. Paul is telling us not to even view or think of our neighbor as wicked or worthless. Paul comes to this conclusion because he knows two things: 1) God doesn't see us as worthless, even with all our dumb decisions, and 2) we treat people per the way we think of them, and it is often connected to how we see ourselves.

In his book, *The Weight of Glory*, C.S. Lewis said, "There are no ordinary people. You have never talked to a mere mortal. Nations, cultures, arts, civilizations-these are mortal, and their life is to ours has the life of a gnat. But it is immortals whom we joke with, work with, marry, snub, and exploit - immortal horrors or everlasting splendors… Next to the blessed sacrament itself, your neighbor is the holiest object presented to your senses."

God sees us as immortal and holy and worthy of all He did to join us back to His side. We were, and are, made in His image and declared very good. If we view our neighbor in any way other than this, we undermine and reject how God sees them and what Jesus did on the cross.

The way we think of our neighbor will guide what we say to them and how we treat them. While it may seem loving to address whatever sin is most apparent, to you, in their life, you'll only ever view them as sinners deserving of punishment. When we see our neighbors as deserving of punishment, we see God as only offering a singular kind of mercy and miss the loving-kindness and compassionate care that He genuinely wants to pour out on them and us.

I know we do this because we've been taught that God's mercy is only the withholding of a punishment that we deserve. Many of us came to Christ with that understanding, and it painted the lens we used to view our neighbor. But you, like them, are recipients of God's compassion and lovingkindness, poured out to relieve your distress. Our neighbors don't need to know what "crime" they've committed that separates them from God. They need to meet the one who shows them mercy. And that is what He's calling us to be witnesses to.

WITNESSES

Recently, within the evangelical movement, there's been a call to "tell people who we're for, not what we're against." That's a great sentiment, and I agree with it, but sadly I think it's born out of a world tired of hearing about Christianity. It's clear, with all the talk of boycotts against certain chicken and pickle sandwiches and craft shops and the heated debates over abortion and same-gender marriage, which the Western world at large doesn't want to hear about Christian moral ethics. I'm not saying we should keep silent on these issues; on the contrary, we should let our beliefs inform how and what we engage in the public square. What I am saying is that we may need to, and probably should rethink our strategy when it comes to going and being Jesus' witnesses to the world.

The Very First Sermon

After the Holy Spirit comes and delivers His power,[16] that Jesus promises as He ascends, Peter steps out and starts preaching. He starts his sermon by saying, "You evil drunkards and adulterers. You perverse prostitutes and men who lay with men. You slack fools, liars, and gossips. Repent of these sins, accept Jesus, and be saved from hellfire." With that right word, the people believed that their ways were evil and responded by accepting Jesus as their Lord and Savior. That day, 3,000 people were added to the church.

Wouldn't that make things easier if that was how his sermon had really gone down? Maybe not easier, but it would surely justify how we approach people today; because isn't that what we've often done when it comes to Jesus? We try to convince people how bad they are and that they deserve hell. And if they don't want to go to Hell, we're ones who have the answer that will get them out of it. It's almost as if we don't trust the power of the Holy

Spirit to convict and compel people, so we need to scare people out of hell and into the Kingdom. But Jesus doesn't want people begrudgingly entering His Kingdom, with fear as their motivation. No, He'd rather see people enter His presence joyfully and without coercion.

If you haven't figured it out, that wasn't the message Peter delivered. Instead, he got up and talked about how Jesus was the One that all scripture points to and how it was Him who God raised to His right hand. Peter preached that Jesus is Christ and Lord and calls the crowd out for killing Him because of their unbelief in Him. He called them to repent of their sin of unbelief[17] that led them to reject Him. He called them to believe in Him. And do you know what happened? Three thousand people were convicted of their unbelief, turned toward Christ, and became followers of Jesus. When was the last time that you saw someone preach condemnation and then have 3,000 people raise their hand to answer the altar call?

The World's Sin

The idea of what sin we are to address, especially when acting as Christ's witnesses, is critical for us to understand. I'm not suggesting that our poor behavior or biblically identified sin shouldn't be our concern. Again, it should be, as long as our sin is our first concern. Likewise, the sin of other Christians should be open for address, but only so long as you've built a relationship that allows for a door into their life. However, when we're talking about the unbeliever and being Jesus' witness, I think we've gotten it drastically wrong.

I've already briefly mentioned John 16:9, but when it comes to addressing the sins of those not found in Christ, we desperately need to understand this verse. It is essential when we consider what Jesus invited us to in the Great Commission and instructed us about being His witnesses. John 16:8-11 reads:

> When [Holy Spirit] comes, He will convict the world about sin, righteousness, and judgment: about sin, because they do not believe in Me; about righteousness, because I am going to the Father and you will no longer see me; and about judgment, because the ruler of this world has been judged.

The context clues in this verse are critical to its understanding. Jesus is saying that the Holy Spirit will come and "convict" the world, meaning He will find fault with and correct and reveal the truth about what they believe about those three things. That means they, the Jews, and we, have misunderstood those things. After identifying the three things we've come to misunderstand, Jesus provides the correct view to which the Holy Spirit will lead the world. In the case of *sin*, Jesus clarifies that the world's first sin is their unbelief in Him. This is an important distinction because it changes the focus of that to which He calls us to be witnesses.

Sin Police

Being a witness isn't easy. Remember how I mentioned how difficult it sometimes was, as a police officer, to get the information I needed from a witness. Apart from the whole, "snitches get stitches" reluctance, witnesses could sometimes be too helpful. What I mean by that is in their attempt at being helpful, they would give information they deemed relevant and not necessarily the information I needed. It convoluted the whole investigative process. Other times they didn't want to be helpful and would withhold information. Other times they would just straight up get the information wrong because they saw it incorrectly or didn't see it at all. All of that is why we depend on multiple witnesses, if possible. I feel like Jesus' witnesses do the same thing. Of course, some just don't want to talk about Jesus. But for the other two: the overly helpful witness and the witness with the wrong perspective, we need to let the Holy Spirit lead us to conviction and clear understanding.

Here's what I mean by that. Both of these types of witnesses get their information wrong in similar ways, but for different reasons. The "wrong perspective witness" focuses on telling the unbeliever what they're doing wrong because they've been taught that bad behavior is what keeps people separated from God. They think it is more important for people to know what the Bible identifies as bad or sinful behavior, rather than addressing the sin with which Jesus is most concerned. Think about it. The whole idea of a secular versus divine divide forces the separation of people into those camps based on behavior and action. We're taught from the beginning of our conversion that we're seeking and saving sinners from hell and bringing them into the Kingdom. It's all based on the bad things that people do. Even our way into the Kingdom is labeled the "Sinner's Prayer" and usually starts with something akin to "I know I'm a sinner and choose turn from my sins." The implication here is that we've made a lot of wrong choices and behaved badly and that we need to admit it so God won't condemn us to Hell. But He didn't say that. Of course, we need to stop doing the things that grieve God, hating others, sexual impurity, etc., but if we're talking about inviting others into the kingdom, our focus has to be the same as Jesus'.

To Go and Do the Same

He came to seek and save the lost. Jesus is looking for those who are perishing because of separation from God and don't know how to get back to Him. Jesus is the one who reconciles our separation. He said He is The Way;[18] as in the way to God. Once Jesus hits the scene, it's the rejection of Him that exaggerates and continues our separation, to the point of our perishing. Romans 10:9-10 is clear that our salvation and justification are entirely based on our confession of and belief in Jesus and his resurrection. We are to confess with our mouths and be saved and believe in our hearts and be justified. Jesus calls us to address people's sin of unbelief. In doing so, the Holy Spirit convicts and leads them out of their unbelief and reveals The Way to God. We are not the "sin police," but rather separation paramedics, bringing the Good News that salves the wounds of the distressed man who is dying on the side of the road. So then, what is the Good News to which we ought to bear witness?

This Is Good News

A few years ago, I tweeted, "The gospel may be offensive, but it never hurts people." Almost immediately, a pastor friend of mine texted me and asked what my scriptural reference was for that claim. I was a little thrown off that that idea was even a questionable one, especially from a pastor. Because he caught off guard, and I know it is always an acceptable answer during any Sunday school lesson, I responded with a sarcastic, "Jesus." But he was serious and wanted a serious reply. Since I value the challenging of ideas as a means of solidifying and even undoing them, I spent the next two weeks studying and working out my premise for the idea that the Gospel doesn't hurt people. If I wanted to be honest with myself and have the idea stand on its own, I had to consider if the Gospel genuinely hurts people? And, was or is it intended to? Here's the answer I came up with and the response I shared with him...

The whole of the gospel can be summed up in John 3:16 - 17. That passage starts, "For God so loved..." Thus the message of the Gospel begins with God's love. God's love is the foundation on which the Good News is built, personified in Christ, realized at the cross, and magnified in His resurrection. The first reality we must grasp is that any attempt to separate or minimize the Gospel from this truth causes it to cease being the Gospel that God delivered to us. A gospel message initiated by anything except Love is not Good News. The fact remains that any Gospel that doesn't start with "For God so loved..." is no Gospel at all.

Three Commands

If then, the Gospel is initiated by and grounded in God's love, what are we to understand about the intent of it concerning the possibility of it hurting us? If God's message of reconciliation to us springs out of His love for us, the only acceptable response to that message has to be love. Jesus explained this in declaring the Greatest Command and the Second Command, which He described as "like it." And if loving our neighbor is like loving God, isn't it likely that we display a tangible expression of our love for God in the love we show for our neighbor? Not only are these the two most important commands, but Jesus also said that the entirety of the law and the prophets are wrapped up in this love thing. Does the love we show our neighbors hurt them? Romans 13:10 says, "Love does no wrong to a neighbor; therefore love is the fulfilling of the law." So no, our love does not hurt our neighbor. And, if our love of God and our neighbor is a mirror response to the love that God initiated His good news with, shouldn't it be that His love does not hurt us?

1 Corinthians 13 explains this clearly. It tells us, "Love is patient and kind; love does not envy or boast; it is not arrogant or rude. It does not insist on its own way; it is not irritable or resentful; it does not rejoice at wrongdoing, but rejoices with the truth. Love bears all things, believes all things, hopes all things, endures all things." Love does not create an environment where hurt can exist. So if the gospel message depends on God's love for humanity, it cannot hurt humankind.

What then, of the offensiveness of the Gospel? This offensiveness is wrapped up in the fact that the love that creates the Gospel message comes against your idea of righteousness. Man's sense of righteousness always focuses on the self. The Gospel means to undo that view by focusing righteousness toward God and others, through Love. This is offensive to your self-righteousness but is still separate from the Good News message. It is also offensive because it seeks to separate you from the sin you so desperately desire to hold close. It calls you out of what offends God and into His view of righteousness, which again causes offense to your "sensibilities" of right and wrong, because "I'm a good person." These are responses to the Gospel and not the Gospel itself. Likewise, any other feelings you have about the Gospel or any reaction to the Gospel is not the Gospel. And, while conviction initiates from the Holy Spirit, spurred on by hearing the Gospel, and may even cause us pain, that again is merely a feeling toward or about the Gospel and the conviction you're experiencing is still not the Gospel.

Consider this. Two men of similar circumstances receive the same Gospel message. One man, being far less emotional, receives the message as logical and surrenders himself to God. For him, it is a rational thing. It may even be a joyful moment. The other man receives the Gospel message and is completely undone by it. He resists it and struggles with how accepting that truth may affect him and what it will likely require of him. It causes him agony, and he probably experiences pain, be it emotional or physical. He eventually and reluctantly surrenders himself to God. In either situation, was the message the same? Yes. Did it intend to hurt either man? No. But one was hurt, and one was not. Why? Was it because of the message or the man's view of it? The Gospel is not a product of your feelings; it's the product of God's Love. And love does no wrong.

This takes us back to the point of what we're called to be witnesses to. Jesus calls us to reveal the truth of who He is and share the Good News that He brought. Again we're not "sin police." We get the Gospel wrong when we choose to tell people about God's anger toward their sin, rather than His love and desire for their reconciliation.

AMBASSADORS

Therefore, we are ambassadors for Christ, certain that God is appealing through us. We plead on Christ's behalf, "Be reconciled to God."
~ 2 Corinthians 5:20 ~

In 2 Corinthians 5:20, the Apostle Paul identifies us as ambassadors for Christ. This is a new role and a little different than being a witness for Him. It's one thing to observe and report or share information about something; you can be completely detached from it while in that role. It becomes quite another thing to represent that same something or someone. That's the precise difference, your connection to the item or person. It's important to know what Paul means by ambassador before we talk about what one does.

What is an Ambassador?

This will require another quick word study lesson. The Greek word that Paul uses was *presbeuo*. *Presbeuo* is the root word for where we get the word *presbyter*, which is essentially an elder of the church. In this case, *presbeuo* means two things, to be older, usually associated with wisdom and knowledge, or to be an ambassador. And ambassador, apart from the political definition attached to it, is an authorized representative or messenger[19] based on knowledge or wisdom of the thing or person you're representing. Paul is telling us that we are authorized representatives of Jesus. The assignment here is far weightier than just being a witness. Jesus isn't going to let us simply tell people about Him without actually representing Him to those to whom we are witnessing. This is about being a disciple, which we've already spelled out. Remember, the disciple was a representative of a rabbi he was committed to learning from and imitating. So imitation is a part of it, but ambassadorship is about far more than imitation. The rabbi's lifestyle became so ingrained that it became the disciple's life. The disciple was then an actual representative, or ambassador, for the rabbi who taught him how to live that particular way. That is our calling as ambassadors of reconciliation.

Sent As Jesus

If we are to be representatives of Jesus, we need to understand what it means to be sent by Him and as Him. In John 17, Jesus prays, for Himself, His disciples, and then all believers. It's a beautiful prayer of thanksgiving, acceptance, protection, and commissioning. In verse 18, Jesus prays, "As you have sent Me into the world, I also have sent them into the world." This verse, in particular, is essential when it comes to our commissioning as disciples. Not that I intend this to be a book of Greek lessons, but it is sometimes necessary to understand what the writer is trying to say. The word for *send* that Jesus uses is *apostello* and is where we get *Apostle*. It means, "to order, by sending away, to an appointed place, usually connected to a specific purpose." In His prayer, Jesus acknowledges that God sent Him to an appointed place and for an appointed purpose. He is sending us, His disciples, in the same way. Our place, the world;[20] our purpose, to appeal, "be reconciled to God."[21]

But, more than just going into the world with a message, we are genuinely being sent as Jesus. Remember, the same spirit that raised Jesus from the dead is living inside of us.[22] Jesus sends us with the same power that enabled Him in everything He did. We are sent as if we are Jesus. I don't mean that to be a blasphemous statement. It's not as if we are the second coming of Christ. I mean, there are enough crazies out there who believe that; I'm not trying to be one of them. What I do mean is that if we are His disciples, and learning to be like our rabbi, by imitating Him, eventually people should see Him in everything we do. It's precisely what Romans 12:2 is talking about when it instructs us to be transformed by the renewing of our mind. As we learn what it means to live and be like Jesus, we eventually transform into His likeness in the way we think and act.

They Have Been With Jesus

We find one of the best examples of this transformation in Acts 4. In Acts 4, we get to see the effects of following Jesus and fellowshipping with other believers. This is a three-year in the making ordeal. The disciples had spent years learning from and imitating Jesus, causing their transformation into His likeness.

After healing a man in the market place and then speaking to the crowd, some people in the group take the Apostles Peter and John to the temple leaders. When they arrive, the leaders "observe their boldness," but realize they are "under-educated and untrained" men, so they were amazed and "recognized they had been with Jesus."[23] Up to this point, neither man had said anything directly to the temple leaders, so it wasn't as if they waxed eloquent about being with Jesus. No, instead, it had to do with everything that led to them being brought before the leaders--healing the lame man in full view of the public and then preaching in the temple with the authority of the Holy Spirit.

Consequently, it wasn't that Peter even showed up there to preach. Peter was just walking around, had an interaction with a man who asked for money, and then accurately estimated and adequately supplied his need. He gave the man what Jesus had given him, wholeness, healing, love, dignity, etc. And it was the man's response, his praising God, which caused people to be in wonder and run over to Peter. Peter then seizes the opportunity to speak about Jesus.

He was operating in his role as an ambassador, representing the life of Jesus, and then witnessed to others about what he knew to be true of Him. And guess what happened? Well, for one thing, he was arrested. But before that, just as every time Peter opened his mouth to talk about Jesus, five thousand people were saved. And that's only the number of men present. That is nothing to say of their wives and children or the other people who worked in their household. In a matter of weeks, two sermons add something close to 20,000, if not more, people to the church. That is what it looks like to be an ambassador.

Jesus told us that if we believe in Him, we will do the work He has done and will, in fact, do even greater.[24] I do believe that He was talking about the miracles He performed, but I also think we place a lot of emphasis on just that work, His signs and wonders. What if He was also talking about all the rest of His life? He's clearly using disciple language here. He's including everything He has done, every act of love and compassion. Every moment of forgiveness and kindness that He offered. He is including every word of truth that He spoke. All of those are His works that we, as ambassadors, will perform to an even greater degree. The first place we get to model these works is in obedience to His command to love each other.

This definition of what it means to be a witness may seem like a departure from the New Command, but it isn't. It's vital to have a clear picture of what being a witness and ambassador means and how they connect to the fulfillment of the Law. These two roles are a direct result of our practice of loving each other and how we invite others into reconciliation with God, so they may join us citizens in His Kingdom. These roles are critical because they are what make us disciple-makers. During Jesus' time, students worked their whole young lives, until early adulthood, intending to follow a specific rabbi. It was a choice they made based on how previous disciples, now their teachers, represented their rabbi. It's the same for us.

How we act as a witness for and represent Jesus will impact people's decision about whether to follow or not to follow Him. We should desire their willing "yes" because we know and have experienced how good God is. Once they say "yes," we lead them into the Kingdom. Then they become part of the church and people we are called to love as part of the New Command, and thus the cycle begins again.

To Go and Do the Same

Three Commands

His Invitation

FINDING LOVE AND LOOKING FOR OTHERS

"Come and follow me, and I will transform you into men who catch people for God."
~ *Jesus* ~

AS WE END THIS JOURNEY, we have some choices. We can continue on our current trajectory, creating Bible studies and service projects that end up just being avenues for allowing people to remain in the Old Covenant. If we continue that process, then we will continue to create tired and burned out cynics. At the very least we continue to create people who are content with attending a Sunday morning lecture that never matures them beyond spiritual milk. Or, we can take Jesus' command to love each other seriously. In doing so, we begin to connect ourselves to a body of believers committed to the practice of loving each other, out of reverence to Jesus. When that happens, we get to experience the fullness of life He promised and gain the ability to love God and our neighbor rightly. From that fullness, we get to invite others in, but more than that, they feel welcome in His Kingdom.

Surely that is the better decision. Of course, making it will take some time and involve a lot of trial and error, but that was the whole reason that the Apostle Paul explained what love looks like in 1 Corinthians 13. This is the only way that you can genuinely experience the love of God and know that He really and truly loves you. I think it's far worse to be a Christian who does not believe God loves them than it is to be a person who doesn't believe in God. When a person decides not to believe in God, they only take on the responsibility to love as best as they can best figure it out. In that case, there's no standard to live up to, except the one they make, and if that standard becomes too challenging to meet, they can adjust to their comfort level.

For a Christian, this isn't the case. They can't change the standard. They also can't meet the standard. The expectation placed on a Christian to "love like God" is an unbearable weight when they don't believe that He loves them the same way. It makes it impossible to love others that way, too. But the good news is, God doesn't expect us to meet His standard for loving others, apart from Him. When we are weak, He is strong.[1] He carries us past the human threshold for loving others. So while the person who doesn't believe in God may seem like they're "off the hook" for loving everyone, they unfortunately also never get to experience the fullness of love, in Christ, that only a unified Christian community can. When we consider the commands of Christ, clarity is essential. All of the other lists of Jesus' commands that others have compiled are important because they are the words of Christ, but none of them carry the same results as obedience to His New Command.

Experiencing the love of Jesus in a genuine and authentic community is what equips us to be His witness in the primary truth, He desires all people to know, His love. If you've not experienced this, then you'll likely find great difficulty in living out His command to love people and then accept His invitation to make and lead disciples to and for Him. And following Him is not a decision we can take lightly. It is more than just a prayer that we say one Sunday morning because someone preached a sermon that drew us to an emotional response. It's a decision that comes at a cost, not just to us, but one that we share with Him. It's a cost that I've learned that I will gladly bear if it means that I get to be with Him. Nabeel Qureshi, the author of *Seeking Allah, Finding Jesus: A Devout Muslim Encounters Christianity*, asked himself a critical question, and it's one we need to consider. He asked, "After loving us with the most humble life and the most horrific death, Jesus told us, "As I have loved you, go and love one another." How could I consider myself a follower of Jesus if I was not willing to live as He lived? To die as He died? To love the unloved and give hope to the hopeless?" It's a weighty question. But take heart, His New Command enables us for all things. His New Command is His invitation to "come follow Me" and to "go make disciples." And when we look at the most important commands that Jesus identified, it was always love: love each other, love God, and love your neighbor. This shows us that at the end of the day, there's only one command that matters: Love.

NOTES

My Invitation
1. 1 John 4:8
2. 1 John 4:20
3. Philippians 1:6

Chapter 1
1. Genesis 1:27
2. Isaiah 6:3
3. John 15:8
4. John 3:16

Chapter 2
1. https://www.biblicalcyclopedia.com/S/simlai-rabbi.html
2. Psalms 119:103, ESV
3. Genesis 1:28, Genesis 3:8, Genesis 4:15
4. Matthew 5:17
5. Jeremiah 3:8
6. 1 John 4:18
7. 2 Corinthians 5:17, Colossians 3:9-10, Romans 6, 2 Corinthians 3:18
8. 2 Peter 1:4

Chapter 3
1. 1 Timothy 1:15
2. 2 Corinthians 5:21
3. 2 Corinthians 11:2
4. 2 Corinthians 11:3
5. *Letters of C.S. Lewis*, p. 231
6. *The Divine Romance*, Gene Edwards, p. 63
7. Matthew 25:40
8. John 15:13
9. *How to Practice Buddhism for Mercy*, Gnanasena Thero
10. Rand, D & Epstien, Z. (2014). Risking Your Life without a Second Thought: Intuitive Decision-Making and Extreme Altruism. *Plos One, 9*(10), 1-6.
11. Matthew 11:28-30
12. Romans 10:9-10
13. 1 John 3:23
14. John 6:29
15. John 13:34
16. John 17:26
17. Colossians 1:15
18. Matthew 11:28-30

Part 2

1. Sh' ma Yisrael - Hear O' Israel, the Lord is our God, the Lord is One, etc.

Chapter 4
1. Bill Gothard, Commands of Christ
2. Evangelist J.S. McConnell, The Commandments of Jesus
3. Matthew 11:30
4. John 15:12
5. John 14:15
6. Matthew 22:40
7. Mark 10:43-45
8. John 13:31-35, Matthew 22:37-40, Romans 13:8-10, Galatians 5:14, James 2:8
9. John 13:34, ESV
10. Mark 10:17-22
11. Romans 10:9
12. Matthew 11:28-30
13. 1 John 3:23
14. 1 John 4:20

Chapter 5
1. My Jewish Learning, https://www.myjewishlearning.com/article/the-shema/
2. Matthew 6:24
3. John 20:24-29
4. John 20:29
5. Acts 4:13
6. John 14:15
7. Colossians 1:15
8. John 21:19
9. 1 John 4:20
10. Philippians 2:8
11. 1 John 4:19
12. Colossians 3:23

Chapter 6
1. Matthew 22:40
2. Mark 12:31
3. Luke 10:29
4. 1 Peter 3:5
5. Romans 10:14
6. John 2:5
7. Luke 10:25-37
8. Matthew 5:39
9. Matthew 5:39
10. Matthew 5:40
11. John 3:3
12. Luke 23:34
13. Matthew 25:40

[14] Do not seek revenge or bear a grudge against anyone among your people, but love your neighbor as yourself. I am the Lord.
[15] 1 Cor 9:25 & 10:13, 1 Thes 5:6, 2 Tim 1:7, Prov 6:32, Prov 25:28, Titus 1:8
[16] Matt 16:24, Prov 25:16, Daniel 1:8, Heb 11:25, Phil 3:7, Matt 5:29, Matt 6:10, Luke 5:27-28, Matt 10:29-30
[17] Ephesians 2:4
[18] Philippians 4:8
[19] Matthew 20:26

Chapter 7
[1] 1 John 4:20
[2] John 1:14
[3] Matthew 6:10
[4] Hebrews 10:24
[5] Ephesians 4:4
[6] John 13:34
[7] 1 Corinthians 1:10, Ephesians 4:13, and John 17:23
[8] Ephesians 4:12
[9] Hebrews 10:24
[10] Proverbs 27:17
[11] Hebrews 10:24-25
[12] 1 John 2:6
[13] Ephesians 4:3
[14] Acts 2:47
[15] Acts 4:13
[16] John 1:1-5
[17] Ephesians 5:21
[18] Ephesians 4:4
[19] Acts 2:46

Chapter 8
[1] John 3:17
[2] Luke 19:10
[3] Matthew 28:18-20
[4] Matthew 28:18
[5] Ephesians 4:12
[6] 2 Corinthians 5:18
[7] Elwell, W.E. (ed.). (2001). *Evangelical Dictionary of Theology* (2 ed.), Grand Rapids, MI: Baker Academics
[8] Ibid
[9] Reformed Perspectives Magazine, 8/2016, vol. 18(33), thirdmill.org/articles/dm_clark/dm_clark.eph04.11.html
[10] Elwell, Gift of Teaching
[11] Acts 6:4
[11] 1 Peter 3:18
[12] Acts 18:8, Galatians 3:26-27, Colossians 2:11-12, Romans 5:3-4
[13] Matthew 28:20
[14] John 15:5
[15] Luke 10:1
[16] Luke 10:17
[17] Matthew 18:20
[18] 1 Corinthians 11:1
[19] Outreach Magazine, Apr 2018, 7 Startling Facts: An Up Close Look at Church Attendance in America, retrieved from ChurchLeaders.com
[20] Matthew 10:26
[21] Matthew 16:25
[22] Romans 8:17
[23] Ephesians 5:22
[24] Philippians 2:3
[25] Ephesians 4:2
[26] Philippians 2:5-9
[27] Philippians 2:17
[28] Matthew 11:28-30
[29] Isaiah 40:31
[30] Matthew 26:69-75
[31] John 13:35
[32] Genesis 3:2-3
[33] Genesis 3:4-5
[34] 2 Corinthians 5:20
[35] Genesis 22:18
[36] Joshua 2
[37] Ruth 1-4
[38] Acts 10:9-16
[39] John 14:15
[40] 1 Peter 4:8
[41] 1 Corinthians 13
[42] 2 Corinthians 5:20
[43] Acts 2:42-47
[44] Hebrews 10:24
[45] Luke 9:24, Mark 10:21, Matthew 19:27-29, Luke 14:26, Matthew 10:38, Matthew 16:24-25
[46] Luke 17:33
[47] Acts 2:41
[48] Acts 2:42, 44, & 46
[49] Acts 2:47
[50] Luke 10:25-37

Chapter 9
[1] Galatians 5:14
[2] Matthew 5:17
[3] John 16:33
[4] Matthew 10:16
[5] John 16:7
[6] John 15 & 16
[7] Psalm 121

Three Commands

[8] Romans 10:14
[9] Ephesians 4:1-6
[10] Romans 10:14
[11] English Standard Version
[12] Romans 3:23
[13] Isaiah 1:11-15
[14] Ecclesiastes 3:17, Hebrews 10:30, Romans 12:19, & Romans 2:6
[15] John 12:49
[16] Acts 2
[17] John 16:9
[18] John 14:6
[19] Definition from Merriam-Webster
[20] John 17:18
[21] 2 Corinthian 5:20
[22] Romans 8:11
[23] Acts 4:13
[24] John 14:12

His Invitation

[1] 2 Corinthians 2:1

www.ingramcontent.com/pod-product-compliance
Lightning Source LLC
Chambersburg PA
CBHW021949290426
44108CB00012B/1005